D0630720

MORAL SCEPTICISM
AND
MORAL KNOWLEDGE

STUDIES IN
PHILOSOPHICAL PSYCHOLOGY

Edited by
R. F. HOLLAND

MORAL SCEPTICISM
AND
MORAL KNOWLEDGE

by
RENFORD BAMBROUGH

HUMANITIES PRESS, INC
ATLANTIC HIGHLANDS, N. J.

*First published in 1979 in England
by Routledge & Kegan Paul Ltd
and in The United States of America
by Humanities Press, Inc.
Atlantic Highlands, N.J. 07716
Set in 10 on 12pt Baskerville by
Computacomp (UK) Ltd, Fort William, Scotland
and printed in Great Britain by
Redwood Burn Ltd, Trowbridge and Esher*

Library of Congress Cataloging in Publication Data

Bambrough, Renford.

Moral scepticism and moral knowledge.
(Studies in philosophical psychology)
Bibliography: p
Includes index.
1. Ethics. I. Title. II. Series.
BJ1012.B36 1979 170 79-13540

ISBN 0-391-01037-9

CONTENTS

ACKNOWLEDGMENTS

My main philosophical debts are acknowledged in the text and the Bibliography.

Professor Roy Holland made numerous helpful comments and suggestions.

I should like to thank Mrs Daphne Field for her skilful and patient secretarial work.

An early version of part of Chapter 2, under the title 'A Proof of the Objectivity of Morals', was published in the *American Journal of Jurisprudence*, 1970 and in *Situationism and the New Morality*, edited by Robert L. Cunningham, New York, 1970.

Renford Bambrough
St John's College, Cambridge

ACKNOWLEDGMENTS

CHAPTER 1

QUESTION

'Just why do you think,' carefully enquired Major Sanderson, the soft and thickset smiling staff psychiatrist to whom the colonel had ordered Yossarian sent, 'that Colonel Ferredge finds your dream disgusting?'

Yossarian replied respectfully. 'I suppose it's either some quality in the dream or some quality in Colonel Ferredge.'

Joseph Heller, *Catch-22*, chapter 27

Yossarian here raises the main question of moral philosophy and aesthetics, and suspends a cautious judgement between the answers most often defended and attacked.

Hume, in *An Enquiry concerning the Principles of Morals*, after first rebuking and dismissing the disingenuous disputants who have altogether denied the reality of moral distinctions, goes on to speak of

a controversy started of late, much better worth examination, concerning the general foundation of Morals; whether they be derived from Reason, or from Sentiment; whether we attain the knowledge of them by a chain of argument and induction, or by an immediate feeling and fine internal sense; whether, like all sound judgement of truth and falsehood, they should be the same to every rational intelligent being; or whether, like the perception of

beauty and deformity, they be founded entirely on the
particular fabric and constitution of the human species.

It is to this question that moral philosophers both before
and after Hume have sought an answer, and the question
and the rival answers have repeatedly been framed in terms
akin to those of Hume. Kant declares in the *Groundwork* (*The
Moral Law*, p. 76) that 'unless we wish to deny to the concept
of morality all truth and all relation to a possible object, we
cannot dispute that its law is of such widespread significance
as to hold, not merely for men, but for all *rational beings as such*
– not merely subject to contingent conditions and
exceptions, but with absolute necessity.' When Hume comes
to answer his own question in Appendix I to the Enquiry (§
234), he gives an important subordinate role to the reason,
but firmly assigns to passions and sentiments, and especially
to the sentiment of *humanity* – one that eponymously belongs
to 'the particular fabric and constitution of the human
species' – the giving of preferences and the production of
moral blame and approbation for qualities and actions
concerning whose several tendencies we may be instructed
by reason. In the *Treatise*, III, i, 2 he speaks of a 'moral sense',
and says that 'Morality, therefore, is more properly felt than
judg'd of '.

There is no need to recite the list of those who have been
of Hume's party or of Kant's, from the sophists and Socrates
to Sartre and Moore. Of greater interest for what follows is to
notice that some moral philosophers, including two of the
greatest, Aristotle and Butler, have given answers that cut
across the neat dichotomy of *nomos* and *phusis*, Hume and
Kant.

Yossarian's words leave the way open for this third type of
answer if we do not insist on taking his 'or' to be exclusive.
Perhaps there must be both some particular quality in the
dream and some particular quality in Colonel Ferredge to
explain why the colonel finds the dream disgusting.

Some words used by Butler in the Dissertation 'Of the Nature of Virtue' show that he was raising the same question and that he was disposed towards this third answer (*The Analogy of Religion*, p. 287):

> It is manifest great part of common language, and of common behaviour over the world, is formed upon the supposition of such a moral faculty; whether called conscience, moral reason, moral sense, or Divine reason; whether considered as a sentiment of the understanding, or as a perception of the heart; or, which seems the truth, as including both.

Bernard, the editor of Butler's works, rightly underlines the significance of Butler's careful choice of words and rightly notes its kinship with the language of Aristotle in the *Nicomachean Ethics*. Butler speaks of a *perception* of the heart and a *sentiment* of the understanding. A lesser editor might have been tempted to emend the text as an editor is said to have improved on Shakespeare by reading 'sermons in books, stones in the running brooks' (*As You Like It*, II, i, 12). Bernard observes instead the fitness of Butler's language to the intricacies of his theme, and the instructive precedent of Aristotle's phrases *orexis dianoētikē* and *orektikos nous* – rational appetite and appetitive reason (*Nicomachean Ethics*, 1139b4–5). He might have added that Hobbes, whose debt to Aristotle, even if less direct, is comparable with Butler's, speaks (though unfavourably) of the 'rational appetite' of the schools.

Hobbes also appropriates and repeats with emphasis a slogan that has for good and ill been part of the common currency of moral philosophy almost since its inception – the tag *intellectus nihil movet*, whose ultimate source is Aristotle's *dianoia outhen kinei* (*Nicomachean Ethics*, 1139a36). Moral theorists have usually been sensitive to accusations of 'intellectualism' even if they were among those who gave primacy to the understanding over the will and the emotions

when faced with a stark dichotomy. Rashdall endorses
Kant's moral rationalism, holding that 'moral approval is a
judgement of the Intellect, not a feeling or an emotion' (*The
Theory of Good and Evil*, vol. I, p. 139), but at once begins to
explain and qualify in anticipation of familiar objections:

> The most obvious form which objections are likely to take
> will be something of this kind: Does not common opinion
> recognize that Morality is an affair, not of the head, but of
> the heart? Are not our moral perceptions attended with a
> glow and warmth of feeling which is entirely absent from
> our perception (say) of a mathematical truth? Are not good
> men very often stupid and bad men often intellectual? If we
> admit that there is an intellectual element in what is
> commonly called Conscience, must we not at least say with
> Bishop Butler that Conscience is neither merely 'a sentiment
> of the understanding' nor 'a perception of the heart,' but
> 'partakes of the nature of both'?

The reference to Butler's dichotomy prepares the way for
a later passage (vol. I, p. 161) in which Rashdall rebukes
two otherwise opposed schools of moral philosophy, whom
he identifies as 'the ordinary Utilitarian' and 'the
rationalistic Moralist' for a joint mistake that they make
when they 'ignore the truth that the content of our moral
judgement is dependent upon the sensitive and emotional as
well as the rational nature of man' or 'fail to take into
account tendencies to particular emotions, spontaneous
tendencies to approve of certain kinds of conduct and to
disapprove of others, which rest upon no logical ground, but
must simply be taken as data upon which the Practical
Reason has to work'. He comes nearer to Hume than some
of his earlier words would suggest when he adds (ibid.):

> The judgement that the tendency of human nature to find
> satisfaction in certain kinds of conduct has value is, indeed,
> an immediate judgement which cannot be derived from
> experience in the ordinary sense of the word; but we very

often cannot say why we should have such a tendency, or deny that in beings differently constituted other kinds of conduct might tend to their highest attainable good.

Hume, for his part, shows some signs of approaching Butler's more complicated account in § 137 of the *Enquiry*, where he describes himself as apt to suspect 'that *reason* and *sentiment* concur in almost all moral determinations and conclusions'. Even Kant wavers at one point and seems at least momentarily to qualify the rigour of his rationalism. He virtually rejects the slogan *intellectus nihil movet* when he writes of the confusions and dangers that beset a *mixed* moral philosophy, one that is compounded of impulsions from feeling and inclination *and* rational concepts, and ascribes to the *pure* thought of duty such power over the human heart that it can dispense with 'empirical inducements' and can master all impulsions from experience and the senses (*The Moral Law*, pp. 78–9). But earlier (pp. 62–3) he has allowed that reason is a feeble goad and guide of appetition, and has made its unfitness for such a role into a ground for ascribing to it, and hence to man, a nobler purpose than the pursuit of happiness, for which instinct and inclination would be more fitting instruments. In the same passage and by the same consideration he explains the 'misology' or mistrust of reason that prompts some gifted and educated men to envy 'the common run of men, who are closer to the guidance of mere natural instinct, and who do not allow their reason to have much influence on their conduct'. Such men may feel that their strenuous reasoning, theoretical as well as practical, seems rather to bring them more trouble than to reward them with happiness or any other advantage.

This has been a cursory consideration of a small number of selected sentences from the history of moral philosophy, but it may nevertheless have served the purpose for which it was undertaken. It shows that the central movement of philosophical debate about morality has been as much concerned with the place of feeling in ethics as with the place of reason in ethics; that indeed the task of moral philosophy has often been seen as the task of determining the respective roles of reason and emotion in moral reflection, judgement and action. No further explanation is needed for the inclusion of a book on the epistemology of morals in a series of Studies in Philosophical Psychology.

But some further explanation can be given. The understanding of the nature of emotion and of the relation between emotion and the understanding is so central to the explanation of the nature of morality as to amount to good reason (though possibly not the particular reason he had in mind) for Professor Richard Wollheim's reported reference to 'that part of the philosophy of mind that is traditionally known as moral philosophy'. I shall argue that morality has repeatedly and almost invariably been misrepresented by theories of ethics, whether subjective or objective, emotivist or intuitionist, and that its correct characterisation calls in particular for the careful description of a kind of utterance whose study is as much a matter for the philosophy of psychology as for moral philosophy itself. If we turn from the theories to a direct description of cases of moral knowledge and judgement, we find that moral knowledge exhibits a peculiarity which is emphasised but variously misrepresented by the rival theorists and which explains how they have been led into their mistakes. We also find that much of the trouble that the theories cause and much of the trouble that causes the theories arises where one theory is in secret and mistaken agreement with another, where because they both agree on a false disjunction each of them sacrifices a truth that the other strenuously guards, and embraces the paradox that it is the primary function of the other to controvert.

If the theories are all wrong, why then pay any attention to the theories at all? It might seem better to be content with the comparisons and descriptions commended by Margaret

Macdonald in her essay on 'Ethics and the Ceremonial Use of Language' (pp. 199–200). But Miss Macdonald herself testifies to the usefulness of the theories, at least by implication, when she contributes her own observations on the nature of moral judgements in the form of a catalogue of some of the merits and defects of some of the theories.

There are grounds for being quite explicit about the advantages of a method that makes use of the traditional theories, and for being quite deliberate and systematic in its application. In the first place, it is not fortuitous that the theories both represent and misrepresent the character of the judgements and disputes of which they are offered as models. It is characteristic of a philosophical enquiry that it should allow, if not require, the dialectical development that is in fact exhibited by traditional moral philosophy. The best argument for this contention is given by applying it to actual texts and problems. In this book I shall confine myself to its concrete application in the sphere of ethics. I expect to be able to show by its use (1) that there is a certain description of the nature of moral disputes on which all the main theories substantially agree and which is substantially correct; (2) that some of the disputes between rival theories are not substantive disputes about the positive character of moral argumentation, but debates about the relative value of a number of standard and recurrent comparisons and contrasts between moral and other modes of understanding; (3) that the disputes about these comparisons and contrasts are resoluble in ways that further contribute to the characterisation of moral knowledge; (4) that the relatively small remainder of stark philosophical conflict between the various theories can be seen in a new light when it is isolated and detached from the considerations that fall under (1), (2) and (3), and can then in its turn be resolved in a way that accounts both for the persistence and for the detailed character of the traditional disputes of moral philosophy and of the theories to which they have given rise.

These traditional theories deserve attention for another reason that has nothing directly to do with epistemology. The theories have often been used for purposes distinct from those of pure philosophy or theory of knowledge. Professor Hare indicates something of the nature of these purposes when he remarks that many of those who defend objectivist theories derive a virtuous glow from the consciousness that they are attacking the wicked relativist or subjectivist ('The Objectivity of Values', p. 4). Hare is quite right about this virtuous glow, though he might have added that it is of the same nature as the virtuous glow felt by the subjectivist or relativist (even perhaps on occasion by the imperativist or prescriptivist) when he attacks the obscurantism of the objective theorist and defends liberal values against the risk of the tyranny and inquisition that objectivism is alleged to further and foster.

Philosophical theories of many other kinds are capable of arousing and expressing emotions akin to these. The reductive philosopher of science wears his operational definitions on his sleeve as proud proof of the toughness of his mind. The conventionalist about logical necessity is comfortably conscious that Occam's razor gives a smooth shave. Their smugness is matched by the Platonist's complacent contempt for their lack of subtlety and their blindness to some things that are in heaven and earth.

These passions and postures are all alike irrelevant to the truth or falsehood of the epistemological theories to which they give rise or respond. Hume's unanswerable rebuke bars any attempt to refute a philosophical theory by predicting that its propagation will have harmful effects (*Treatise*, II, iii, 2):

> There is no method of reasoning more common, and yet none more blameable, than in philosophical debates to endeavour to refute any hypothesis by a pretext of its dangerous consequences to religion and morality. When any opinion leads us into absurdities, 'tis certainly false; but 'tis

not certain an opinion is false, because 'tis of dangerous
consequence. Such topics, therefore, ought entirely to be
foreborn, as serving nothing to the discovery of truth, but
only to make the person of an antagonist odious.

But such a reaction to a theory is as likely as the theory itself
to point to an aspect or element in morality that has been
overlooked, or at least to a difficulty that needs an answer.
And it may have the further utility, which no
epistemological theory as such can have, of raising or
helping to answer questions of substantive morality that
have been disguised as or confused with philosophical
questions about morality.

   An important group of questions of this kind is centred on
the concepts of sincerity, integrity and authenticity, and on
related concepts such as those of self-knowledge, self-deceit
and self-control; spontaneity, freedom and compulsion,
knowing what one is doing, intention, motive and will.
These concepts are of intrinsic philosophical interest, and
are often studied by philosophers under one or both of the
headings of philosophical psychology or moral psychology.
It is not my purpose in this book to offer a systematic or
comprehensive account of all or any of them, but they are
germane in two main ways to my enquiry into the nature of
moral knowledge:

   (1) It is by rightly insisting on their importance while
wrongly construing their implications that many moral
philosophers from Protagoras to Sartre have been led into
some of the most persuasive but most misguided of
subjectivist accounts of moral reasoning.

   (2) The corrected account of these concepts that restores a
juster perspective to our picture of moral enquiry can also
contribute to the first hand moral understanding to whose
pursuit the subjectivist or existentialist has sought, self-
defeatingly, to sacrifice the very possibility of objective moral
progress.

   It can, for example, make clear whether Kant and Tolstoy

were right in the confidence they placed in the moral consciousness of the ordinary man, and whether any scope is left, once we have ratified the autonomy of morals, for the exercise of moral authority, or for moral advice and instruction; and hence any role for the wise man, sage or pundit, any ground for legal, moral or political coercion of the individual by Parliament or Pope or scientific expert.

Yet the main theme and the main purpose of this book are epistemological. Its aim is to show that 'the ordinary moral consciousness' is right in regarding itself as a *consciousness*, as an awareness of things that are not dependent for their existence or properties upon the fact of being apprehended. Such an epistemological conclusion has lessons to offer to those who are also concerned with the philosophical treatment of substantive moral and political issues, and some of them will be outlined or hinted at when they are visible from the path of the epistemological investigation.

The first step along that path is to offer a direct proof of the objectivity of morals, and hence to undertake to show that the familiar arguments for moral subjectivism, however popular and persuasive, are necessarily ill-founded.

CHAPTER 2

PROOF

When Hamlet or Macbeth reasons with himself about
suicide or murder we can see for ourselves which are the pros
and which are the cons, and what force and weight they
carry. Macbeth is Duncan's kinsman and his subject, strong
both against the deed. Then, as his host, he should against
the murderer shut the door, not bear the knife himself.
Besides, this Duncan does not deserve a tyrant's death. He
has been clear in his great office; his taking-off would be a
deep damnation, and his virtues would plead against it like
angels trumpet-tongued. Hamlet needs to consider not only
the Almighty's canon, fixed against self-slaughter, but also
the danger that to sleep may be perchance to dream. This
mortal coil is at least mortal, however heavy the burdens it
brings from the law's delays and the insolence of office.

When a philosopher reasons with us about knowledge of
good and evil, we may lose our grip on this knowledge and
understanding. A lack of realism besets us in this as in other
philosophical disputes, so that moral knowledge, like any
other kind of knowledge, becomes prey to philosophical
scepticism. Moral scepticism has often tempted philosophers
whose understanding of the sources and grounds and
functions of sceptical doctrines generally might have been
expected to protect them against the bewitchment of a
scepticism so extravagant that Hume declines to discuss it
(*Enquiries*, § 133):

Those who have denied the reality of moral distinctions, may be ranked among the disingenuous disputants; nor is it conceivable, that any human creature could ever seriously believe, that all characters and actions were alike entitled to the affection and regard of everyone. The difference, which nature has placed between one man and another, is so wide, and this difference is still so much farther widened, by education, example, and habit, that, where the opposite extremes come at once under our apprehension, there is no scepticism so scrupulous, and scarce any assurance so determined, as absolutely to deny all distinction between them. Let a man's insensibility be ever so great, he must often be touched with the images of Right and Wrong; and let his prejudices be ever so obstinate, he must observe, that others are susceptible of like impressions. The only way, therefore, of converting an antagonist of this kind, is to leave him to himself. For, finding that nobody keeps up the controversy with him, it is probable he will, at last, of himself, from mere weariness, come over to the side of common sense and reason.

It is well known that recent British philosophy, under the leadership of Moore and Wittgenstein, has defended common sense and common language against what seem to many contemporary philosophers to be the paradoxes, the obscurities and the mystifications of earlier metaphysical philosophers. The spirit of this work is shown by the titles of two of the most famous of Moore's papers: 'A Defence of Common Sense' and 'Proof of an External World'. It can be more fully but still briefly described by saying something about Moore's defence of the commonsense belief that there are external material objects. His proof of an external world consists essentially in holding up his hands and saying, 'Here are two hands; therefore there are at least two material objects.' He argues that no proposition that could plausibly be alleged as a reason in favour of doubting the truth of the proposition that I have two hands can possibly be more certainly true than that proposition itself. If a philosopher produces an argument against my claim to *know* that I have two hands, I can therefore be sure in advance that *either* at least one of the premises of argument is false, *or* there is a mistake in the reasoning by which he purports to derive from his premises the conclusion that I do not know that I have two hands.

Moore himself speaks largely in terms of knowledge and belief and truth and falsehood rather than of the language in which we make our commonsense claims and the language in which the sceptic or metaphysician attacks them, but his procedures and conclusions are similar to those of other and later philosophers who have treated the same topic in terms of adherence to or departure from common language. A so-called linguistic philosopher would say of the sceptic that he was using words in unusual senses, and that when he said that we do not know anything about the external world he was using the word 'know' so differently from the way in which we ordinarily use it that his claim was not in conflict with the claim that we make when we say that we *do* know something about the external world. Moore takes the words of the sceptic literally, and shows that what he says is literally false. The linguistic philosopher recognises that what the sceptic says is literally false, and goes on to conclude that the sceptic, who must be as well aware as we are that what he says is literally false, is not speaking literally. Both Moore and the linguistic philosopher maintain with emphasis (Moore is famous for his *emphasis*) that we literally *do* know of some propositions about the external world that they are true; they both hold fast to common sense and common language.

It is also well known that many recent British philosophers have rejected objectivist accounts of the nature of moral reasoning. The most famous and fashionable of recent British moral philosophers, while they differ substantially in the detail of their accounts of moral judgements and moral reasoning, agree in drawing a sharp contrast between moral reasoning on the one hand, and mathematical, logical, factual and scientific reasoning on the other hand. They sharply contrast *fact* with *value*. They attach great importance to Hume's doctrine, or what they believe to have been Hume's doctrine, that *is* never entails *ought*, that from no amount of factual evidence does any evaluative proposition logically follow; that no set of premises about what is the case, unless they are combined with at least one premise about what is good or what ought to be the case, can yield any conclusion about what is good or what ought to be the case. While simple and extreme subjectivism is seldom explicitly defended nowadays, simple and extreme objectivism is almost never defended. Most of the fashionable doctrines, with the great stress that they lay on the emotive, prescriptive and imperative functions of moral propositions, lean so far towards the subjectivist end of the scale that they are sometimes, and naturally, lumped together under the title of 'the new subjectivism'. We are repeatedly told that there are no moral *truths*, that there is no moral *knowledge*, that in morals and politics all that we can ultimately do is to *commit* ourselves, to declare where we stand, to try by persuasion and rhetoric to bring others to share our point of view.

A speaker at the Cambridge Moral Sciences Club not many years ago began a paper on moral philosophy by saying that he would assume that we all agreed that all forms of objectivism must be rejected, and he was so used to swimming with a full tide that he was obviously and sincerely surprised, not to say slightly shocked, to find that there were some people present who would not allow him to take this agreement for granted.

What is apparently not very well known is that there is a conflict between the fashionable allegiance to common sense and common language and the fashionable rejection of objectivism in moral philosophy.

I have no doubt that the philosopher I have just referred to, and many of those who agree with him about moral philosophy, would accept Moore's argument, or something closely akin to it, as a conclusive argument in favour of the claim that we have knowledge of the external world.

Many contemporary British philosophers accept Moore's proof of an external world. Many contemporary British philosophers reject the claim that we have moral knowledge. There are some contemporary British philosophers who both accept Moore's proof of an external world and reject the claim that we have moral knowledge. The position of these philosophers is self-contradictory. If we can show by Moore's argument that there is an external world, then we can show *by parity of reasoning*, by an exactly analogous argument, that we have moral knowledge, that there are some propositions of morals which are *certainly* true, and which we *know* to be true.

My proof that we have moral knowledge consists essentially in saying, 'We know that this child, who is about to undergo what would otherwise be painful surgery, should be given an anaesthetic before the operation. Therefore we know at least one moral proposition to be true.' I argue that no proposition that could plausibly be alleged as a reason in favour of doubting the truth of the proposition that the child should be given an anaesthetic can possibly be more certainly true than that proposition itself. If a philosopher produces an argument against my claim to *know* that the child should be given an anaesthetic, I can therefore be sure in advance that *either* at least one of the premises of his argument is false, *or* there is a mistake in the reasoning by which he purports to derive from his premises the conclusion that I do not know that the child should be given an anaesthetic.

When Moore proves that there is an external world he is defending a commonsense belief. When I prove that we have moral knowledge I am defending a commonsense belief. The contemporary philosophers who both accept Moore's proof of an external world and reject the claim that we have moral knowledge defend common sense in one field and attack common sense in another field. They hold fast to common sense when they speak of our knowledge of the external world, and depart from common sense when they speak of morality.

When they speak of our knowledge of the external world they not only do not give reasons for confining their respect for common sense to their treatment of that single topic but assume and imply that their respect for common sense is *in general* justified. When they go on to speak of morality they not only do not give reasons for abandoning the respect for common sense that they showed when they spoke of our knowledge of the external world, but assume and imply that they are still showing the same respect for common sense. But this is just what they are *not* doing.

The commonsense view is that we *know* that stealing is wrong, that promise-keeping is right, that unselfishness is good, that cruelty is bad. Common language uses in moral contexts the whole range of expressions that it also uses in non-moral contexts when it is concerned with knowledge and ignorance, truth and falsehood, reason and unreason, questions and answers. We speak as naturally of a child's not knowing the difference between right and wrong as we do of his not knowing the difference between right and left. We say that we do not know what to do as naturally as we say that we do not know what is the case. We say that a man's moral views are unreasonable as naturally as we say that his views on a matter of fact are unreasonable. In moral contexts, just as naturally as in non-moral contexts, we speak of thinking, wondering, asking; of beliefs, opinions, convictions, arguments, conclusions; of dilemmas, problems, solutions; of perplexity, confusion, consistency and inconsistency, of errors and mistakes, of teaching, learning, training, showing, proving, finding out, understanding, realising, recognising and coming to see.

I am not now saying that we are right to speak of all these

things as naturally in one type of context as in another, though that is what I do in fact believe. Still less am I saying that the fact that we speak in a particular way is itself a sufficient justification for speaking in that particular way. What I am saying now is that a philosopher who defends common sense when he is talking about our knowledge of the external world must *either* defend common sense when he talks about morality (that is to say, he must admit that we have moral knowledge) *or* give us reasons why in the one case common sense is to be defended, while in the other case it is *not* to be defended. If he does neither of these things we shall be entitled to accuse him of inconsistency. I do accuse such philosophers of inconsistency.

Moore did not expect the sceptic of the senses to be satisfied with his proof of an external world, and I do not expect the moral sceptic to be satisfied with my proof of the objectivity of morals. Even somebody who is not a sceptic of the senses may be dissatisfied with Moore's proof, and even somebody who is not a moral sceptic may be dissatisfied with my proof. Even somebody who regards either proof as a conclusive argument for its conclusion may nevertheless be dissatisfied. He may reasonably wish to be given not only a conclusive demonstration of the truth of the conclusion, but also a detailed answer to the most popular or plausible arguments against the conclusion.

Those who reject the commonsense account of moral knowledge, like those who reject the commonsense account of our knowledge of the external world, do of course offer arguments in favour of their rejection. In both cases those who reject the commonsense account offer very much the same arguments whether or not they recognise that the account they are rejecting is in fact the commonsense account. If we now look at the arguments that can be offered against the commonsense account of moral knowledge we shall be able to see whether they are sufficiently similar to the arguments that can be offered against the commonsense account of our knowledge of the external world to enable us to sustain our charge of inconsistency against a philosopher who attacks common sense in one field and defends it in the other. (We may note in passing that many philosophers in the past have committed the converse form of the same *prima facie* inconsistency: they have rejected the common-sense account of our knowledge of the external world but have accepted the commonsense account of moral knowledge.)

'Moral disagreement is more widespread, more radical and more persistent than disagreement about matters of fact.'

I have two main comments to make on this suggestion: the first is that it is almost certainly untrue, and the second is that it is quite certainly irrelevant.

The objection loses much of its plausibility as soon as we insist on comparing the comparable. We are usually invited to contrast our admirably close agreement that there is a glass of water on the table with the depth, vigour and tenacity of our disagreements about capital punishment, abortion, birth control and nuclear disarmament. But this game may be played by two or more players. A sufficient reply in kind is to contrast our general agreement that this child should have an anaesthetic with the strength and warmth of the disagreements between cosmologists and radio astronomers about the interpretation of certain radio-astronomical observations. If the moral sceptic then reminds us of Christian Science we can offer him in exchange the Flat Earth Society.

But this is a side issue. Even if it is true that moral disagreement is more acute and more persistent than other forms of disagreement, it does not follow that moral knowledge is impossible. However long and violent a dispute may be, and however few or many heads may be counted on this side or on that, it remains possible that one party to the

dispute is right and the others wrong. Galileo was right when
he contradicted the cardinals; and so was Wilberforce when
he rebuked the slave-owners.

There is a more direct and decisive way of showing the
irrelevance of the argument from persistent disagreement.
The question of whether a given type of enquiry is objective
is the question whether it is *logically capable* of reaching
knowledge, and is therefore an *a priori*, logical question. The
question of how much agreement or disagreement there is
between those who actually engage in that enquiry is a
question of psychological or sociological fact. It follows that
the question about the actual extent of agreement or
disagreement has no bearing on the question of the
objectivity of the enquiry. If this were not so, the objectivity
of every enquiry might wax and wane through the centuries
as men become more or less disputatious or more or less
proficient in the arts of persuasion.

*'Our moral opinions are conditioned by our environment and
upbringing.'*

It is under this heading that we are reminded of the
variegated customs and beliefs of Hottentots, Eskimos,
Polynesians and American Indians, which do indeed differ
widely from each other and from our own. But this objection
is really a special case of the general argument from
disagreement, and it can be answered on the same lines. The
beliefs of the Hottentots and the Polynesians about
straightforwardly factual matters differ widely from our
own, but that does not tempt us to say that science is
subjective. It is true that most of those who are born and
bred in the stately homes of England have a different outlook
on life from that of the Welsh miner or the Highland crofter,
but it is also true that all these classes of people differ widely
in their factual beliefs, and not least in their factual beliefs
about themselves and each other.

The moral sceptic's favourite examples are often presented as though they settled the issue beyond further argument.

(1) Herodotus reports that within the Persian Empire there were some tribes that buried their dead and some that burned them. Each group thought that the other's practice was barbarous. But (a) they agreed that respect must be shown to the dead; (b) they lived under very different climatic conditions; (c) we can now see that they were guilty of moral myopia in setting such store by what happened, for good or bad reasons, to be their own particular practice. Moral progress in this field has consisted in coming to recognise that burying-versus-burning is not an issue on which it is necessary for the whole of mankind to have a single, fixed, universal standpoint, regardless of variations of conditions in time and place.

(2) Some societies practice polygamous marriage. Others favour monogamy. Here again there need be no absolute and unvarying rule. In societies where women heavily outnumber men, institutions may be appropriate which would be out of place in societies where the numbers of men and women are roughly equal. The moralist who insists that monogamy is right, regardless of circumstances, is like the inhabitant of the Northern Hemisphere who insists that it is always and everywhere cold at Christmas, or the inhabitant of the Southern Hemisphere who cannot believe that it is ever or anywhere cold at Christmas.

(3) Some societies do not disapprove of what we condemn as 'stealing'. In such societies, anybody may take from anybody else's house anything he may need or want. This case serves further to illustrate that circumstances objectively alter cases, that relativity is not only compatible with, but actually required by, the objective and rational determination of questions of right and wrong. I can maintain that Bill Sykes is a rogue, and that prudence requires me to lock all my doors and windows against him,

without being committed to holding that if an Eskimo takes whalemeat from the unlocked igloo of another Eskimo, then one of them is a knave and the other a fool. It is not that we disapprove of stealing and that the Eskimos do not, but that their circumstances differ so much from ours as to call for new consideration and a different judgement, which may be that in their situation stealing is innocent, or that in their situation there is no private property and therefore no possibility of *stealing* at all.

(4) Some tribes leave their elderly and useless members to die in the forest. Others, including our own, provide old-age pensions and geriatric hospitals. But we should have to reconsider our arrangements if we found that the care of the aged involved for us the consequences that it might involve for a nomadic and pastoral people: general starvation because the old could not keep pace with the necessary movement to new pastures; children and domestic animals a prey to wild beasts; a life burdensome to all and destined to end with the early extinction of the tribe.

'When I say that something is good or bad or right or wrong I commit myself, and reveal something of my attitudes and feelings.'

This is quite true, but it is equally and analogously true that when I say that something is true or false, or even that something is red or round, I also commit myself and reveal something of my *beliefs*. Emotivist and imperativist philosophers have sometimes failed to draw a clear enough distinction between what is said or meant by a particular form of expression and what is implied or suggested by it, and even those who have distinguished clearly and correctly between meaning and implication in the case of moral propositions have often failed to see that exactly the same distinction can be drawn in the case of non-moral propositions. If I say 'this is good' and then add 'but I do not approve of it', I certainly behave oddly enough to owe you an explanation; but I behave equally oddly and owe you a comparable explanation if I say 'that is true, but I don't believe it.' If it is held that I contradict myself in the first case, it must be allowed that I contradict myself in the second case. If it is claimed that I do not contradict myself in the second case, then it must be allowed that I do not contradict myself in the first case. If this point can be used as an argument against the objectivity of morals, then it can also be used as an argument against the objectivity of science, logic, and of every other branch of enquiry.

The parallel between *approve* and *believe* and between *good* and *true* is so close that it provides a useful test of the paradoxes of subjectivism and emotivism. The emotivist puts the cart before the horse in trying to explain goodness in terms of approval, just as he would if he tried to explain truth in terms of belief. Belief cannot be explained without introducing the notion of truth, and approval cannot be explained without introducing the notion of goodness. To believe is (roughly) to hold to be true, and to approve is (equally roughly) to hold to be good. Hence it is as unsatisfactory to try to reduce goodness to approval, or to approval plus some other component, as it would be to try to reduce truth to belief, or to belief plus some other component.

If we are to give a correct account of the logical character of morality we must preserve the distinction between appearance and reality, between seeming and really being, that we clearly and admittedly have to preserve if we are to give a correct account of truth and belief. Just as we do and must hope that what we believe (what seems to us to be true) is in fact true, so we must hope that what we approve (what seems to us to be good) is in fact good.

I can say of another, 'He thinks it is raining, but it is not,' and of myself, 'I thought it was raining, but it was not.' I can also say of another, 'He thinks it is good, but it is not,' and of myself, 'I thought it was good, but it was not.'

'After every circumstance, every relation is known, the
understanding has no further room to operate, nor any object on
which it could employ itself.'

This sentence from the first Appendix to Hume's *Enquiry Concerning the Principles of Morals* is the moral sceptic's favourite quotation, and he uses it for several purposes, including some that are alien to Hume's intentions. Sometimes it is no more than a flourish added to the argument from disagreement. Sometimes it is used in support of the claim that there comes a point in every moral dispute when further reasoning is not so much ineffective as impossible in principle. In either case the answer is once again a firm *tu quoque*. In any sense in which it is true that there may or must come a point in moral enquiry beyond which no further reasoning is possible, it is in that same sense equally true that there may or must be a point in *any* enquiry at which the reasoning has to stop. Nothing can be proved to a man who will accept nothing that has not been proved. Moore recognises that his proof of an external world uses premises which have not themselves been proved. Not even in pure mathematics, that paradigm of strict security of reasoning, can we *force* a man to accept our premises or our modes of inference; and therefore we cannot force him to accept our conclusions. Once again the moral sceptic counts as a reason for doubting the objectivity of morals a feature of moral enquiry which is exactly paralleled in other departments of enquiry where he does not count it as a reason for scepticism. If he is to be consistent, he must either withdraw his argument against the objectivity of morals or subscribe also to an analogous argument against the objectivity of mathematics, physics, history, and every other branch of enquiry.

But of course such an argument gives no support to a sceptical conclusion about any of these enquiries. However conclusive a mode of reasoning may be, and however accurately we may use it, it always remains possible that we shall fail to convince a man who disagrees with us. There may come a point in a moral dispute when it is wiser to agree to differ than to persist with fruitless efforts to convince an opponent. But this by itself is no more a reason for doubting the truth of our premises and the validity of our arguments than the teacher's failure to convince a pupil of the validity of a proof of Pythagoras's theorem is a reason for doubting the validity of the proof and the truth of the theorem. It is notorious that even an expert physicist may fail to convince a member of the Flat Earth Society that the earth is not flat, but we nevertheless *know* that the earth is not flat. Lewis Carroll's tortoise ingeniously resisted the best efforts of Achilles to convince him of the validity of a simple deductive argument, but of course the argument *is* valid.

> '*A dispute which is* purely *moral is inconclusive in principle. The specifically* moral *element in moral disputes is one which cannot be resolved by investigation and reflection.*'

This objection brings into the open an assumption that is made at least implicitly by most of those who use Hume's remark as a subjectivist weapon: the assumption that whatever is a logical or factual dispute, or a mixture of logical and factual disputes, is necessarily *not* a moral dispute; that nothing is a moral dispute unless it is *purely* moral in the sense that it is a dispute between parties who agree on *all* the relevant factual and logical questions. But the *purely moral* dispute envisaged by this assumption is a pure fiction. The search for the 'specifically moral element' in moral disputes is a wild-goose chase, and is the result of the initial confusion of supposing that no feature of moral reasoning is *really* a feature of moral reasoning, or is *characteristic* of moral reasoning, unless it is peculiar to moral reasoning. It is as if one insisted that a ginger cake could be fully characterised, and could only be characterised, by saying that there is ginger in it. It is true that ginger is the peculiar ingredient of a ginger cake as contrasted with other cakes, but no cake can be made entirely of ginger, and the ingredients that are combined with ginger to make ginger cakes are the same as those that are combined with chocolate, lemon, orange or vanilla to make other kinds of cakes; and ginger itself, when combined with other ingredients and treated in other ways, goes into the making of ginger puddings, ginger biscuits and ginger beer.

To the question 'What is the place of reason in ethics?' why should we not answer: 'The place of reason in ethics is exactly what it is in other enquiries, to enable us to find out the relevant facts and to make our judgements mutually consistent, to expose factual errors and detect logical inconsistencies'? This might seem to imply that there are some moral judgements which will serve as starting points for any moral enquiry, and will not themselves be proved, as others may be proved by being derived from them or disproved by being shown to be incompatible with them, and also to imply that we cannot engage in moral argument with a man with whom we agree on *no* moral question. In so far as these implications are correct they apply to all enquiry, and not only to moral enquiry; and they do not, when correctly construed, constitute any objection to the rationality and objectivity of morality or of any other mode of enquiry. They seem to make difficulties for moral objectivity only when they are associated with a picture of rationality which, though it has always been powerful in the minds of philosophers, can be shown to be an unacceptable caricature.

Here again the moral sceptic is partial and selective in his use of an argument of indefinitely wide scope: if it were true that a man must accept unprovable moral premises before I could prove to him that there is such a thing as moral knowledge it would equally be true that a man must accept an unprovable material object proposition before Moore could prove to him that there is an external world. Similarly, if a moral conclusion can be proved only to a man who accepts unprovable moral premises then a physical conclusion can be proved only to a man who accepts unprovable physical premises.

'There are recognised methods for settling factual and logical disputes, but there are no recognised methods for settling moral disputes.'

This is either false, or true but irrelevant, according to how it is understood. Too often those who make this complaint are arguing in a circle, since they will count nothing as a recognised method of argument unless it is a recognised method of logical or scientific argument. If we adopt this interpretation, then it is true that there are no recognised methods of moral argument, but the lack of such methods does not affect the claim that morality is objective. One department of enquiry has not been shown to be no true department of enquiry when all that has been shown is that it cannot be carried on by exactly the methods that are appropriate to some other department of enquiry. We know without the help of the sceptic that morality is not identical with logic or science.

But in its most straightforward sense the claim is simply false. There *are* recognised methods of moral argument. Whenever we say 'How would you like it if somebody did this to you?' or 'How would it be if we all acted like this?' we are arguing according to recognised and established methods, and are in fact appealing to the consistency requirement to which I have already referred. It is true that such appeals are often ineffective, but it is also true that well-founded logical or scientific arguments often fail to convince those to whom they are addressed. If the present objection is pursued beyond this point it turns into the argument from radical disagreement.

The moral sceptic is even more inclined to exaggerate the amount of disagreement that there is about methods of moral argument than he is inclined to exaggerate the amount of disagreement in moral belief as such. One reason for this is that he concentrates his attention on the admittedly striking and important fact that there is an ,enormous amount of immoral *conduct*. But most of those who *behave* immorally appeal to the very same methods of moral argument as those who condemn their immoral conduct. Hitler broke many promises, but he did not explicitly hold that promise-breaking as such and in general was permissible. When others broke their promises to him he complained with the same force and in the same terms as those with whom he himself had failed to keep faith. And whenever he broke a promise he tried to *justify* his breach by claiming that other obligations overrode the duty to keep the promise. He did not simply deny that it was his duty to keep promises. He thus entered into the very process of argument by which it is possible to condemn so many of his own actions. He was *inconsistent* in requiring of other nations and their leaders standards of conduct to which he himself did not conform, and in failing to produce *convincing reasons* for his own departures from the agreed standards.

Here we may remember Bishop Butler's remark that the true standard of morality can be found by noticing what 'every man you meet puts on the show of', however true it may be that not all men live up to their pretensions (*The Analogy of Religion*, p. 287).

The same point can be illustrated in national politics. When the Opposition complain against an alleged mis-demeanour on the part of the Government, they are often reminded that they themselves, when they were in office, behaved in the same way in similar circumstances. They are then able to reply by pointing out that the *then*

Opposition complained vigorously in the House of
Commons. In such cases both sides are proceeding by
recognised methods of argument, and each side is convicted
of inconsistency by appeal to those methods.

So far I have been defending a particular type of account
of moral enquiry against a number of objections. I maintain
that the account I have defended is the commonsense
account, and that it can be defended against philosophical
attacks in the manner in which Moore's commonsense
account of our knowledge of the external world can be
defended against philosophical attacks. At this point a new
question arises. If I am right in claiming that my account is
in accordance with common sense and common language,
why has it been so vigorously attacked, and why in particular
has it been attacked by philosophers who pride themselves
on their fidelity to common sense and common language?
We can find the key to the solution of this problem if we look
further at Moore's treatment of our knowledge of the
external world and at the sceptical objections against which
he defended it.

After attending to Moore's defence of common sense and
his proof of an external world we may ask, 'Why in that case
do so many philosophers maintain that common sense is
mistaken, and that we do not in fact know anything about
the external world?' The situation appears more puzzling
still when we notice that Moore does not claim to be telling
the sceptics anything that they do not already know. He
propounds what has been called 'Moore's paradox', that
sceptical philosophers themselves know as well as Moore
does that their conclusions are untrue.

When this puzzlement becomes more articulate it may
take a rather different form. We may say, 'Surely Moore
must be *missing the point* of the arguments of the sceptical
philosophers. If they know as well as he does that we *do* have
knowledge of the external world, then they cannot seriously
mean to deny that we have knowledge of the external world.

When they seem to deny what they and all of us very well know, they must really be doing something else, and we must not rest content with showing that what they *say* is false. Perhaps what they *say* is not what they *mean*.' And this is what some philosophers have said about scepticism and Moore's answer to it. John Wisdom has described Moore's procedure as 'legalistic'. While Moore is quite right in his arguments and in his conclusions, many of his readers remain dissatisfied, because they feel that his convincing disproof of the sceptical conclusion needs to be supplemented by a fuller account of the sources and motives and effects of scepticism.

We must ask, 'What is the point that Moore is missing? If the sceptic, under the guise of doubting our claim to have knowledge of the external world, is really doing something else, what else is he really doing?' He is portraying the character of our knowledge of the external world by implicitly contrasting our knowledge of the external world with our knowledge of mathematics and our knowledge of our own minds. When he explicitly claims that we have no knowledge of the external world he is implicitly claiming that our knowledge of the external world is different in kind from these other forms of knowledge. He *says* that no proposition about the external world is certainly true: he *means* that no proposition about the external world has the same *kind* of certainty as some propositions about minds or some propositions of mathematics.

If we now return to the moral sceptic we can see that what he was doing was to draw implicit comparisons and contrasts between moral knowledge and other kinds of knowledge. When I defended the commonsense view that we *do* have moral knowledge, I was being 'legalistic', as Moore was being legalistic when he defended the commonsense view that we have knowledge of the external world. In any sense in which he was missing the point of the sceptic of the senses, I was in the same sense missing the point of the moral

sceptic. And just as the sceptic of the senses is not finally
disposed of by showing that what he says is literally false, so
the moral sceptic is not finally disposed of by showing that
what he says is literally false. Each of them makes by his
paradox a point which is quite compatible with the platitude
that his paradox literally denies. But just as Moore rightly felt
it worthwhile to demonstrate to the sceptic of the senses that
his paradox *was* a literal denial of a platitude, because he
suspected that the sceptic was not fully aware of the nature
of his own procedure, so I have felt it worthwhile to
demonstrate to the moral sceptic that his paradox is a literal
denial of a platitude, because I suspect that many moral
sceptics, even if they are fully aware that scepticism of the
senses is the denial of a platitude, are not fully aware that
moral scepticism is the denial of a platitude.

In moral philosophy, as in the philosophy of perception,
to demonstrate the falsehood of scepticism and the un-
soundness of sceptical arguments is an important beginning, but it is only a beginning. It needs to be followed
by a positive exposition and description of the character of
the knowledge that the sceptic declares not to deserve the
name of knowledge, and an explanation of how its character
prompts the sceptic to propound his paradoxes, and hence
of how his paradoxes contribute to our understanding of its
character.

To give an account of what the moral sceptic *means* that is
right, i.e. to give an account of the peculiarity of moral
judgements that gives rise to sceptical paradoxes, is nothing
like so easy and straightforward a thing to do as the
preliminary task of showing that what the sceptic *says* is false
and that the arguments by which he tries to establish what he
says have false premises or invalid steps. And this is just what
we have learned to expect of a long-standing philosophical
dispute. If a dispute is capable of being settled by the presentation of a memorable theory or by a briefly manageable
description then it is almost certainly not a philosophical

dispute and it is quite certainly not a long-standing philosophical dispute. The paradoxical doctrines and the unsound sceptical arguments abound precisely because there is no way of describing the peculiarity of moral judgements that is brief and accurate and memorable.

Fortunately there is another side to this close connection between the informal complexity of the character of morality and the paradoxes of ethical theory: since the paradoxes are manifestations of conscious or unconscious recognition of the existence and nature of the peculiarity, they can to some degree contribute to the direct description of morality and not only, as I have already hinted, to the presentation of its character by the indirection of portrait or caricature.

What is clearest is the sceptic's recognition of the *existence* of a peculiarity. Every one of his arguments is presented or may be re-presented as an alleged point of contrast between morality and some other form of understanding. As each supposed contrast is shown to fail, the area within which we are to look for what differentiates moral from factual or logical reasoning is correspondingly narrowed, while at the same time the positive description of moral reasoning itself is extended over an increasing range of points of *comparison* with other modes of thought. But the sceptic's consciousness that there *is* a peculiarity is so clear that even when he persistently fails to identify or describe it he will not abandon the search, and will sometimes be prepared to embrace new paradoxes and even manifest contradictions rather than to sacrifice his initial and increasingly discredited formulation.

There is one well-known moral philosopher who has repeatedly been heard in discussion to pursue a line of thought which clearly illustrates the causes and effects of this phenomenon. He first announces, in opposition to some intuitionist or objectivist doctrine, that morality is prescriptive and not cognitive. He supports this thesis by the standard succession of contrasts, but is led to accept that every remark he makes about the character of morality is also applicable to natural science; and in the end he says that science too is prescriptive or subjective: 'To say that a scientific proposition is true is in the last resort to say that it is accepted by the scientists of our culture circle.' He thus loses the point of his original remark, which was to *contrast* morality (explicitly or implicitly) with science. He is contradicting his initial claim that morality is different and hence agreeing with his objectivist critic that science and morals are in the same boat.

There is still the question of which boat that is, but progress has been made when the irrelevant points about disagreement and cultural differences have been cleared away. A more important step that becomes possible at the same stage is to distinguish, as the sceptic himself almost never does, between those of his arguments that are specific to morality, or to evaluation, and those that are of unlimited range, and can be used, if at all, against any mode of knowledge or enquiry. All forms of moral scepticism that rely only or mainly on the alleged impossibility of answering a moral question without first or *ipso facto* laying down some standard or criterion or foundation of morality are applications to morality of sceptical considerations of wide general scope which have no special relevance to morals. These considerations must be firmly separated from the specific factors of specifically moral scepticism to whose presence in the compound a sceptic testifies if he persists in his moral scepticism even when he has allowed that all the arguments I have so far discussed have as much or as little force against science or logic as against morality.

Many of the forms of moral scepticism that are special cases of sceptical theories of potentially wider scope are based on confusions between the concepts of relativity and subjectivity and those of absoluteness and objectivity. To suggest that there is a *right* answer to a moral problem is at once to be accused of or credited with a belief in moral absolutes. But it is no more necessary to believe in moral absolutes in order to believe in moral objectivity than it is to believe in the existence of absolute space or absolute time in order to believe in the objectivity of temporal and spatial relations and of judgements about them.

The trouble here is partly due to a recurrence of the difficulty about criteria or standards which, as we have seen, has as much or as little force as a sceptical argument in moral as in non-moral contexts. If we think of the objectivity of ethics as being bound up with the possibility of stating unexceptionably correct rules or moral principles, we shall be liable to regard the evident fact that circumstances alter cases as a refutation of objective theories. The confusion may be dispelled by looking at some closely comparable cases which nevertheless offer no temptation to any analogous confusion. The fact that a tailor needs to make a different suit for each of us, and that no non-trivial specification of what a suit has to be like in order to fit its wearer will be without exceptions, does not mean that there are no rights and wrongs about the question whether your suit or mine is a good fit. On the contrary: it is precisely because he seeks to provide for each of us a suit that will have the *right* fit that the tailor must take account of our individualities of build. In pursuit of the objectively correct solution of his practical problem he must be decisively influenced by the relativity of the fit of clothes to wearer.

Similar examples may be indefinitely multiplied. Children of different ages require different amounts and kinds of food; different patients in different conditions need different drugs and operations; the farmer does not treat all his cows or all his fields alike. Circumstances objectively alter cases.

Some of the cases that are objectively altered by circumstances are cases calling for moral choice or judgement. If we need examples we can find them in the sceptic's own armoury of differences of moral practice and belief between one time or place and another. In collecting them he makes one of his many indirect and inadvertent contributions to the objective description of the objectivity of moral thought. When he reminds us that the ancient Greeks exposed unwanted children and left them to die, whereas we place them in orphanages or have them adopted, he does not, as he thinks, point to a clear case of conflict of moral belief. The effect of his citing such an instance is to open an investigation into the facts and circumstances of ancient Greek life, and how they compare and contrast with those of modern life, and a debate about whether the differences are such as to justify a difference of practice. If they are, then it will have turned out that in spite of superficial appearances there is no moral conflict between the ancients and ourselves. If there turns out to be a residual conflict, large or small, it may be that part of the difference is accounted for by differences in non-moral belief. If a man believes that a finite and temporal torment is the only way of saving a heretic from infinite and eternal torment, he may be prompted by motives of charity to reinforce his reasoning with the rack. And we may believe that charity would require the use of the rack in such circumstances without believing that such circumstances have ever arisen or could ever arise. Our disagreement with the Inquisitor, which is represented by the moral sceptic as an irresoluble dispute about moral principles, is then seen to be a dispute which, whether resoluble or not, is not about fundamental moral principles, but about the truth or falsehood of some non-moral propositions – historical, psychological and theological. A related point is elegantly made by Sir David Ross in a comment on Professor Ayer's emotive theory (*Foundations of Ethics*, p. 38):

> I conclude, then, that the latest attempt to discredit ethics is not successful. Indeed, there is one of the arguments put forward by the positivists which seems to me to provide, when reflected on, an argument in favour not only of the view that our ethical judgements are genuine judgements,

but of the view that there are fundamental ethical
judgements for which general agreement may be claimed.
Mr Ayer remarks that, while his theory escapes many of the
objections brought against subjectivistic theories in ethics,
there is one which it does not escape. This is the argument
that such theories would make it impossible to argue about
questions of value, which nevertheless we undoubtedly do.
He admits that his own theory also would make it impossible
to argue about questions of value; as he holds that such
sentences as 'thrift is a virtue' and 'thrift is a vice' do not
express propositions at all, he clearly cannot hold that they
express incompatible propositions. If, then, he is to resist the
argument in question, he must simply deny that in fact we
ever do dispute about questions of value; for if we did
dispute about things which on his theory we cannot dispute
about, his theory would clearly be untrue. He boldly adopts
the course to which he is logically forced, and denies that we
ever do dispute about questions of value. And he justifies this
by saying that apparent disputes about questions of value are
really disputes about questions of fact.

As Ross remarks on the next page, Ayer's emphasis on the
extent to which our disagreements in ethics turn on
questions of consequences, motives and other matters of
fact, serves to underline our agreement in our fundamental
moral judgements:

for unless we thought that if we could agree on the factual
nature of the act we should probably agree on its rightness
or wrongness, there would be no point in trying to reach
agreement about its factual nature. And in the great
majority of cases we find this confidence confirmed, by
finding that we agree in our moral judgements when we
agree about the facts.

Some of the writings of William James, and especially his
essays 'The Will to Believe' and 'The Sentiment of
Rationality', illustrate how difficult it is to retain a firm hold
on the objectivity and rationality of philosophy, religion and

morals if one is also trying to do justice both to what James calls the 'personal contribution' that a man makes to his acts and judgements and to the manifold variety of human beings and their circumstances. James is right to point out that a philosophy fit for Bismarck 'will almost certainly be unfit for a valetudinarian poet', but wrong to suppose that this fact limits the scope for the application of reason to morals and philosophy of life. Whether a given mode of life fits or fails to fit the temperament and circumstances of Bismarck or of Proust is a question calling as much as any other for a sober judgement. James's own example makes the point he is trying to deny, since he recognises and expects the reader to recognise that it would be a *mistake* to expect of the poet what it is reasonable to expect of Bismarck, and wrong to condemn Bismarck for lacking what the poet may show of delicacy, sensitivity, or a kind of self-knowledge that is understandably rarer in vigorous men of action than in the cloister and the garret. And it happens that the use of the words 'fit' and 'unfit' takes us back to the example of the tailor by which I sought earlier to illustrate the distinction between relativity and subjectivity.

Rashdall shows in his chapter on 'Vocation' in Volume II of *The Theory of Good and Evil* that he recognises the scope for a 'personal contribution', and hence a sense in which morality is relative: that what is morally to be expected of a person, e.g. in the choice of his career, is relative to his talents, circumstances and inclinations. But he sees that this relativity does not compromise the rationality or objectivity of moral choice and judgement. On the contrary, in order to take account of the complexities of individual circumstances one needs to apply one's mind carefully and judiciously, with intelligence and detachment. Rashdall thinks that A. E. Taylor may have made too much of the idea of Vocation (pp. 138–9):

He seems to me to go much too far when he says that such a

problem as that of Isabella in *Measure for Measure*, called upon to choose between her chastity and her brother's life, is 'altogether a problem for the agent herself to decide, and to decide by reference to her own personal feelings.' It may be quite true that 'what might in one woman be an act of heroic self-sacrifice might in another be a cowardly desertion of duty'; that would be in all probability because of the partial knowledge which each would possess of the circumstances and consequences of her act, and of like acts, upon general Well-being; or because, though the ideal of each might have much in it that is valuable, one or both of them may have been more or less imperfect and one-sided.

The same point is seen and trenchantly expressed by Bradley, who inveighs against 'the common error that there is something "right in itself" for me to do, in the sense that either there must be some absolute rule of morality the same for all persons without distinction of times and places, or else that all morality is "relative", and hence no morality' (*Ethical Studies*, 2nd edn, p. 189).

Bradley denies that there is any such 'fixed code or rule of right', but he also denies that such a code or rule is needed for the underwriting of morality (ibid.):

> It is abundantly clear that the morality of one time is not that of another time, that the man considered good in one age might in another age not be thought good, and what would be right for us here might be mean and base in another country, and what would be wrong for us here might there be our bounden duty. This is clear fact, which is denied only in the interest of a foregone conclusion. The motive to deny it is the belief that it is fatal to morality. If what is right here is wrong there, then all morality (such is the notion) becomes chance and convention, and so ceases. But 'my station and its duties' holds that *unless* morals varied, there could be no morality; that a morality which was *not* relative would be futile, and I should have to ask for something 'more relative than this'.

CHAPTER 3

INTEGRITY

The division of the case against objective theories into six distinct objections has necessarily suffered from an element of arbitrariness. The objections and the answers overlap and criss-cross in various ways, and different distinctions and connections might have been considered. But there is one limitation of my list that is deliberate and reasoned. I have reserved for separate treatment an objection which is usually felt to have special if not conclusive force against objectivism; and I have done so not only because of its importance, but also because the attempt to answer it marks the beginning of the positive characterisation of moral enquiry which I wish to add to the answers to objections.

This seventh objection is expressed by P. H. Nowell-Smith when he remarks that 'It is no accident that religious persecutions are the monopoly of objective theorists' (*Ethics*, p. 47). William James makes the same objection to 'the doctrine of certitude' (i.e. to the idea that knowledge is obtainable in moral and religious contexts) when he alleges that one of its clearest consequences has been 'the conscientious labors of the Holy Office of the Inquisition' (*The Will to Believe and Other Essays*, p. 17). R. M. Hare echoes James and Nowell-Smith when he rebukes Professor Geach for accepting the Aristotelian view that man has a function (*ergon*), a view which, Hare says, led Aristotle to tolerate the institution of slavery and the subjection of women ('Geach: Good and Evil', p. 82).

The suggestion is that if we believe (as Hume does) that there *are* moral distinctions (Right and Wrong, Good and Evil) we shall become dogmatic and authoritarian, and that, in the light of that assumption, we shall have reason for our authoritarian principle and practice.

The clearest sign that the objection is misguided is that it falls foul of Hume's rebuke, quoted on pp. 8–9, to those who try to refute a philosophical thesis by arguing that its acceptance will lead to harmful consequences. It does so by way of a confusion that needs separate diagnosis and treatment. All three objectors make use of *moral* premises in their arguments against an *epistemological* thesis. Like the sceptic of the senses, who finds it natural to employ the argument from illusion, these moral sceptics use in their argumentation against a whole species of enquiry a proposition which itself belongs to that enquiry, and whose credentials as an object of knowledge cannot be exempted from the scope of any objection brought against that enquiry as a whole. The argument from moral illusion is no more sound than the argument from perceptual illusion, and Nowell-Smith's mistake can be exposed by giving further consideration to the parallel between the two arguments.

Let us suppose that Moore, when presenting his proof of an external world to the British Academy, held up an object that he took from an inside pocket, and said 'Here is a pencil'. Let us imagine that with all his customary emphasis Moore insisted that he *knew* that he had a pencil in his hand. And suppose that the object was in fact not a pencil but a pen. The sceptic in the front row would find the debating point irresistible. There is a story that once when Moore was lecturing in the United States he pointed to a curtain and said 'I know that there is a window in that wall', though in fact there was no window, but only a curtain covering a blackboard. But in all such cases the sceptic defeats his own argument, and establishes the case for his opponent; for the effect of his riposte is to provide his opponent with an example of just the type that he was seeking, even if (inadvertently, or perhaps cunningly) he did not at first present an example of the type that his argument needs.

Nowell-Smith and Hare and James are hoist with the same petard. Persecution, inquisition and slavery function in their arguments as moral villainies that the objectivist's moral philosophy requires him to countenance. They see themselves as pointing out to the objectivist that he has made a moral mistake. They accordingly see themselves as correcting that mistake, as the sceptic of the senses corrects the mistake of one who sees as an oasis what is only a mirage, as a bent stick what is really a straight stick in water. But a mistake cannot be corrected or even made in a sphere in which there is no right or wrong or true or false. Our recognition that slavery and tyranny and persecution are morally objectionable is a sample of the moral knowledge that the critics' conclusion declares to be impossible, even while their premises openly exemplify it.

Besides relying on an explicit moral premise which is irrelevant to his epistemological conclusion, Nowell-Smith also relies on an implicit causal premise which is equally irrelevant to it. He supposes that those who believe that there is such a thing as moral knowledge will be liable to be dogmatic in their moral judgements, and, if they have power or authority, to be authoritarian and domineering in its exercise. If this were true, it would be a causal, psychological truth, having no logical bearing on the truth or falsehood of Nowell-Smith's subjectivist epistemology of morals. In general, it is possible for p and q to be logically independent propositions, and yet for a belief in p to be liable, psychologically, to be accompanied by a belief in q. But such a psychological phenomenon is of no use to us when our interest is in the truth or falsehood of p and/or of q.

What is more serious for Nowell-Smith is that it does not even seem to be true that those who are most confident that there is such a thing as moral knowledge either have or think they have any reason to lean towards dogma and a domineering disposition. Once again the point can be put most economically by making the necessary comparison between ethics and science.

John Stuart Mill's resounding statement of the principle of free and open enquiry makes no distinction between opinions on one kind of question and opinions on another: 'If all mankind minus one were of one opinion, and only one person were of the contrary opinion, mankind would be no more justified in silencing that one person than he, if he had the power, would be justified in silencing mankind.' (Mill, *On Liberty*, chapter II).

If we are to understand the bearing of this declaration on questions about disagreement in ethics we need to remember that Mill had reasons for it, and did not offer it, as some of his successors have been tempted to do, as an arbitrary postulate or self-evident principle. We need also to remember what his reasons were. He believed in freedom of scientific enquiry because he believed that the establishment and dissemination of scientific truth would be hampered by any form of censorship, repression, or inquisition, and by the imposition of any orthodoxy, however certainly true the content of its creed might be. The same reason has the same force and points to the same conclusion when we apply it to freedom of expression about questions of morals, politics, philosophy and religion. The man who is in a minority of one may be right, and that is why, or is at least one of the main reasons why, it is important not to suppress his opinion.

Mill was himself an objectivist in moral philosophy, and he rightly saw no conflict between his objectivism and his liberalism. On the contrary, his belief that knowledge was obtainable was here again one of the grounds of his adherence to the principle of free enquiry. Suppression of opinion and enquiry and criticism is objectionable because it leads to the maintenance of illusion and the propagation of errors.

Hare crosses the wires and muddies the waters when he tries to treat science and morals differently in this respect: according to him 'we are free to form our own moral opinions in a much stronger sense' than that in which we are free 'to form our own opinions on such matters as whether the world is round' (*Freedom and Reason*, p. 2). What is this sense or species of freedom that belongs to the moral judge and not to the scientist? Hare cannot be suspected of wishing to differentiate between them in degree of liberty of thought, expression and enquiry. What he seems to mean is that in ethics, unlike science, we are not restricted on pain of irrationality to arriving at such and such a conclusion after dispassionately considering the relevant arguments and evidence. In ethics we may also claim the freedom to determine what *is* relevant to the question at issue, whereas in logic and science the meaning of the terms of a question and the relevance or irrelevance of a given consideration or datum or premise are outside our control.

No convincing reason has been given, by Hare or by any other philosopher, for the supposed distinction. A useful step towards giving convincing reasons against it is to notice its kinship with the thesis of James and Nowell-Smith that objectivism about moral questions is logically linked with dogmatism, tyranny and inquisition. Hare is afraid that if it is allowed or recognised that morality is as fully rational as science or logic, we shall in some unwelcome sense be *forced* to draw moral conclusions when faced with moral evidence and moral argument; that the cogency of moral argument might amount to a morally repugnant form of compulsion or coercion.

These anxieties can be stilled by uncrossing the wires. My freedom of scientific thought, expression and enquiry is not limited by the fact that sometimes I am faced with strong or even conclusive evidence in favour of a particular conclusion, even if the conclusion is so unwelcome to me that in one good sense of the words I accept it against my will. And though there is a good sense in which I may *refuse* to accept even a conclusion that is in this other sense 'forced' upon me, this point again applies equally to moral and to non-moral conclusions. Stubbornness, wilful ignorance, perversity and self-deception are not limited to any one sphere of influence.

It is the objective theorist of morals who has the strongest reason to favour freedom of moral enquiry, just as it is the physicist or astronomer, who believes that answers to questions of physics and astronomy are in principle obtainable and establishable, who sees the greatest merit in freedom of scientific enquiry. To claim that there is such a thing as knowledge, or knowledge of such and such a kind, is not to claim to possess such knowledge, or to claim the right to impose one's opinion on others or to suppose that the possession of knowledge would confer such a right. If any theory in the epistemology of morals does give colour to dogmatism and the exercise of tyrannical authority it is a subjective theory, according to which nothing is objectively wrong, and hence the exercise of tyranny is not objectively wrong. It is Nowell-Smith himself who makes the mistake of seeing a link between objectivism and dogmatism, since it is he and not the objectivist who overlooks the possibility, which is open to us in ethics and politics and religion as well as in science and history and logic, of recognising our ignorance and aspiring after knowledge. Where there is no possibility of knowledge there is no scope for ignorance either. I may recognise number theory and genetics as branches of knowledge without claiming even an elementary understanding of them. My recognition of morality as a branch of knowledge does not commit me to the claim that I have much or any moral understanding.

The logical independence between a moral proposition and an epistemological proposition, on which I have relied in my argument against Nowell-Smith, can be supported by noticing that epistemology is the study of questions and how to answer them. The epistemology of morals asks such questions as 'How, if at all, can I know that persecution is wrong?', and the philosophy of perception asks such questions as 'How, if at all, can I know that I am seeing an oasis and not a mirage?' But to study these questions is *ipso facto* to study the questions 'How, if at all, can I know that persecution is *not* wrong?' and 'How, if at all, can I know that I am seeing a mirage and not an oasis?' For these are simply alternative versions of the same questions. The question 'Is it the case that p?' and the question 'Is it the case that not p?' and the question 'Is it or is it not the case that p?' are all versions of the same question. Since the epistemology of any of them is therefore the epistemology of all of them, it is not to be expected that an epistemological characterisation of them, and of the procedures for resolving them, will itself support any particular answer to any of these questions.

Though we are concerned here with abstract issues of epistemology, they are directly relevant to substantive moral issues, as can be shown by an example which also serves as a first step towards the positive characterisation of morality that we are seeking. It is a true story of an incident at an American university some years ago. A graduate student was expelled from the university, and it was believed by other students that he had been expelled for living with a woman student on the campus. At once there was a protest parade with banners declaring that 'Morality is a matter of private choice'. Later it was rumoured that the expulsion had been imposed as a penalty for gross and persistent blackmail of a member of the faculty. The protest died: there were no banners proclaiming that 'Blackmail is a matter of private choice'.

By retiring from the protest the students confirmed what had always been obvious, that they certainly did not believe that morality is a matter of private choice, and that their protest was itself a moral protest. They were complaining at what they regarded as the immorality of interference by academic authorities in some aspects of their private lives. There were other forms of interference that they were prepared morally to countenance. And so their formulation of their protest was doubly misconceived. They were not defending free choice over the whole range of their own conduct but only over some particular part or parts of the range; and their protest against what they took to be the actions and attitudes of the authorities was itself a moral protest, supported by moral feeling, moral argument, and by at least the threat of moral sanctions. Nobody was arguing that the morality of interference in the private choices of others was a moral issue that could in its turn be left to private choice.

The same incoherence, arising from the same sources, is clearly visible in the contrast between the answers of students to questions of moral philosophy and the reactions of student audiences to popular political speakers and causes. At Berkeley in the spring of 1967 I saw two striking instances of this phenomenon. Dr Martin Luther King, speaking on the steps of Sproul Hall on 17 May, referred to suggestions that by joining the opposition to the Vietnam war he had weakened the civil rights movement; and to suggestions that he had joined the opposition to the war only because by doing so he could strengthen the civil rights movement. People were always telling him that it would be safer or more politic or more popular to take this stand or that, or to refrain from taking this or that stand. 'But', he said with rising emphasis and to a chorus of six thousand cheers, 'I do not take any stand because I think it is safe, or because I think it is politic, or because I think it will be popular: when I take a stand, I take a stand because I think it is *right*.' Most of the same throats were hoarse again four days later. Senator Wayne Morse, in a similarly emphatic and effective anti-war speech on the same steps on 21 May, evoked the same response: 'People will tell you that the Vietnam issue is a purely strategic issue, or that it is a purely economic issue, or that it is a purely political issue. But I tell you that it is not just a strategic issue, or an economic issue, or a political issue: it is a *moral* issue.' At least five thousand of those cheering voices could have been persuaded, and many would have needed no persuasion, to agree in philosophical discussion that nothing is good or bad but thinking makes it so.

One of the most explicitly sceptical moral philosophers is Bertrand Russell, who often noticed but never accounted for the paradoxical tension between his scepticism and the passion of his attachment to moral and political causes. In the course of a controversy with T. E. Hulme, who wrote in the *Cambridge Magazine* under the pseudonym of 'North Staffs', he adds to his substantive moral argument against the First World War some comments on the epistemology of morals (Hulme, *Further Speculations*, pp. 211–12):

> On the abstract question of ethics which North Staffs seeks to raise, I do certainly mean to maintain that *all* ethics is subjective, and that ethical agreement can only arise through similarity of desires and impulses. It is true that I did not hold this view formerly, but I have been led to it by a number of reasons, some logical, some derived from observation. Occam's Razor, or the principle that constructions are to be substituted for inferred entities wherever possible, leads me to discard the notion of absolute good if ethics are to be accounted for without it. Observation of ethical valuations leads me to think that all ethical valuations can be so accounted for, and that the claim of universality which men associate with their ethical judgements embodies merely the impulse to persecution or tyranny.

Russell here commits himself to the confusion that we have already found in Nowell-Smith as well as in the students of two American universities. For him, too, the claim to offer moral conclusions whose rightness or wrongness is independent of men's wishes and desires and choices 'embodies merely the impulse to persecution and tyranny'. In the same passage he makes use of other considerations that repeatedly enter into debates about the objectivity of morals. He supposes, as many subjectivists do, and as too many of their opponents have been prepared to accept, that the objectivity of moral enquiry is bound up with the 'absoluteness' of moral rules or principles, with a kind of 'universality' that will involve us in imposing on the actual complexities of life and conduct, motive and circumstance, a rigid, cramping, stultifying simplicity. Bradley and Rashdall are two of the few philosophers of either party who have kept clear heads about the distinction between absoluteness and objectivity, between the subjective and the relative.

In all these examples trouble arises from failing to notice the distinction between two things that might be meant by saying that there is knowledge of a certain kind. It is parallel to an ambiguity in the question whether there is a proof of a particular mathematical theorem. There is a proof that the square on the hypotenuse of a right-angled triangle is equal to the sum of the squares on the adjacent sides. The theorem was proved by Pythagoras. That it was proved by Pythagoras, or at all, is a matter of contingent historical fact. But it is not a contingent matter that what Pythagoras offered *is* a *proof* of the theorem. If the proposition had been logically incapable of being proved, Pythagoras could not have proved it. When *he* asked, before finding his proof, 'Is there a proof of this proposition?' he was not asking the contingent question 'Has anybody proved this proposition?' He was working on the problem because he knew that nobody had produced a proof. His question and his answer were mathematical, not historical.

When I argue that there is such a thing as moral knowledge I am liable to be misunderstood as claiming that I myself, or some authority that I could identify and describe, possess such knowledge or at least the means of access to it. Plato believed that there was such a thing as moral knowledge, and he also believed that it was accessible to his philosopher-kings, and hence that he was justified in imposing their authority on the other citizens of his ideal city. But it is possible to share Plato's conviction that morality is an objective branch of enquiry, whose conclusions are capable of being known to be true, without believing *either* that the main content of the moral knowledge that we seek has been found, *or* that the possession of it would justify us in imposing our wills on those who are ignorant of it.

The question 'Is there such a thing as moral knowledge?', when the words express a need for epistemological understanding, is just as *a priori* as the question 'Is there a proof of this proposition?' when it is asked by a mathematician *mathematically*, and not as a question about what the historical record will show. The only arguments that can be brought for or against this version of the thesis that there is moral knowledge will have to do with the logical relations between moral propositions and other propositions, moral concepts and other concepts. It is by exploring logical space that we shall determine whether there is the theoretical possibility of achieving the knowledge that Plato believed himself and his rulers to have attained.

My disagreement with Plato is largely confined to the question whether the possession of moral knowledge qualifies and entitles a ruler to rule, even against the will of his subjects, and the related question whether moral knowledge is a specialised *technē* like medicine or mathematics. I agree with him that there is such a thing as moral knowledge, in the epistemological sense of those words. And I also agree with him that there is *actual* moral knowledge. We all possess some moral knowledge and understanding, and could not engage in moral controversies if we did not. Without it we could not even engage in controversies about whether, in the epistemological sense, there is moral knowledge. It is, to use Nowell-Smith's own phrase, 'not an accident' that his critique of moral objectivism reveals his own moral understanding that persecution and tyranny are wrong.

But Nowell-Smith could be an objectivist and still be a liberal – like Mill. There is nothing illiberal in the belief that some opinions are right and others wrong, in morals or in any other sphere. To argue for or against liberalism is implicitly to recognise the truth of objectivism, and this is made specially plain by the argument of Nowell-Smith and of the rebellious students, that because moral opinions are subjective it is *wrong* to interfere in people's lives.

The contradiction is so stark that it calls for explanation. Here again there is a parallel between the moral sceptic and the sceptic about perception. In both cases we must look for *to aition tou pseudous* – the reason for the mistake – because that will also, as Aristotle points out, help us to establish the truth that has been obscured.

Scepticism of the senses is made plausible by the character of the knowledge that it challenges: it is only through the senses that we have knowledge of the existence and nature of an external world, and hence that knowledge appears vulnerable to the sceptic's observation that a conclusion about the existence of material things does not follow from any set of premises about sensory experiences. The task for the philosopher of perception, once he is armed with Moore's proof, is to account for the plausibility of the sceptic's argument and to reconcile it with the falsehood of the sceptic's conclusion. The task of the moral philosopher has the same structure, once we have reached the same stage in the exploration of moral knowledge. In this case, too, to know the source of the plausibility of scepticism is to begin to understand the character of the knowledge against which it is directed. We must therefore seek, and may have confidence that we can find, a description of moral knowledge which will reconcile its status as knowledge with the sceptic's persuasive emphasis on the requirement of moral freedom, authenticity and autonomy. This central element in morality cannot be denied and must not be obscured; like the role of experience in our knowledge of the external world, it can be incorporated in an account that does justice to the sceptic's argument without tempting us to compromise with his conclusion.

When all these preliminary investigations have been completed as carefully as possible, so that the covert in which the peculiarity of moral judgement lurks has been more narrowly circumscribed, there is still no brief formula that will identify or describe it in the general terms beloved of philosophers and their readers. And if it were possible accurately to describe it briefly and in general terms, the words of the formula or description would still need to be clarified and elaborated by the only method in which this or any philosophical lesson can be satisfactorily taught or learned: by the detailed presentation, in terms that borrow nothing from the language of philosophical theories, of a number of typical and non-controversial examples of the species of propositions whose nature is in question: not by explanation but by description.

CHAPTER 4

DESCRIPTION

In the Preface to the *Sermons*, Butler suggests that it would be better if philosophers never offered conclusions, but only premises. The thought is echoed in some of Wittgenstein's remarks: that in philosophy we should abjure all explanation, and that description alone should take its place; that if one were to offer theses in philosophy they would be of no interest because nobody would want to deny them. Wisdom reports that when he told Wittgenstein that a conversation with another philosopher had not gone well, Wittgenstein said to him 'Perhaps you made the mistake of denying something that he asserted.'

No philosophers, not even Butler and Wittgenstein, have consistently followed this advice, which, like all good advice, is easier to give than to take. But philosophers have offered premises as well as conclusions, descriptions as well as theories and explanations; and if we attend to their descriptions while temporarily disregarding the theories that they were designed to support, we find that there is greater unanimity about the detailed character of morality than the slogans and labels would lead us to expect, and that the partisan theorists have already done for us the greater part of what needs to be done by way of 'aseptic' description.

But before we test this expectation against the descriptions offered by some ethical theorists, we shall do better still to look directly at some examples of what they were intending to describe; to see for ourselves whether we can identify in typical cases of judgements of value any distinguishing feature that sets them apart from typical cases of judgements of other kinds.

Outside an office that I occupied for one quarter at Berkeley, California, there used to be heard from time to time a tired, bored voice, amplified by a loudspeaker van, commending the menu of a restaurant in downtown Oakland, and urging us all, in particular, not to miss its 'absolutely delectable tossed French salads'. Italics would misrepresent the tone of the injunction. It was clear that the speaker had either never felt or had long forgotten the delight that those salads were said to hold in store for us. Neither in his voice nor in his heart was there any of the joy that the use of the word 'delectable', taken by itself, would lead us to expect, and which the owner of the restaurant was hoping and paying to transmit from that heart and voice to ours.

The advertiser of salads from a loudspeaker van, like the author of a lapidary inscription, is not on oath. We may exempt him, as we exempt the actor, from the requirement to feel what his words purport to express. But even the actor and the advertiser are expected by their patrons or employers to put into their voices what may be absent from their hearts, and if we compare and contrast these cases with that of a friend who recommends to us the delectable tossed French salads at Joe's place we find that the role of the feeling is put into higher relief. The actor and the advertiser might be said to commit a licensed insincerity. An unworldly colleague of mine therefore merely amused his guests when he said to them: 'I'm surprised you didn't like the charcoal biscuits. They were extremely well spoken of in the advertisement.' If somebody who carries no such licence says that the salads are delectable without feeling and/or without seeming to feel the delight that the word betokens, in questioning his sincerity we question his right to say what he has said. We accuse him of not meaning what he says, and so show our recognition that the feeling and its expression have a connection with the meaning of his words that they would not have had if he had been offering us only information about the size or price of a salad at Joe's place.

The same idiosyncratic aspect of evaluative judgements may be seen in the fact that a value judgement is ordinarily assumed to be a first-hand judgement, based on the speaker's own direct acquaintance with and reaction to the object of the judgement, unless there is a specific indication to the contrary. If you ask me which is the best play in London at the present time, I may tell you that it is the new play by Edward Albee. If you later see the play and find it disappointing, you will perhaps say to me 'I don't know what you saw in it.' It will not do for me then to explain that I have not seen the play myself, and that my advice was based on the remarks of friends and the reports of the critics. If I have not seen the play I ought to have said in the first place 'I'm told it's very good,' or 'It's said to be good, but I haven't seen it.'

But in all these cases the question of whether what is said is *true* is independent of whether it is sincerely meant by the speaker. My friend may be quite right or quite wrong about the salads at Joe's place or the play at the Haymarket Theatre.

It would be a mistake to think that the point involved here is concerned only or mainly with the rarity and the consequent unexpectedness of the occurrence of such a word in the absence of the relevant reaction or response. This can be shown by considering another example. I may surprise you very much, because I exhibit a very rare reaction or lack of reaction, if I tell you, in the flat tone used by the hawker of salads, that I have just won £200,000 in a football pool. But here it is evident that the meaning and the truth conditions of my claim are not directly called in question by the oddity of my response. I may be able to establish positively by the appropriate evidence that what I say is true. My right to say that I have won that sum of money in that way is not affected by the gloom or indifference with which I tell you so.

If I say in the same gloomy or indifferent tone that I am thrilled and delighted at my success, the case is altered. My right to use these words may be directly questioned if in the utterance of them there is no perceptible trace of a thrill of delight.

If Colonel Ferredge finds Yossarian's dream disgusting, there is some quality in the Colonel. If the dream *is* disgusting there is some quality in the dream. When the dream is disgusting and the Colonel finds it disgusting there is some quality in the dream and some responsive quality in the Colonel.

The truth of the content of a belief is ordinarily independent of any question about the integrity or sincerity or authenticity of the believer's affirmation. This is more clearly illustrated if we take as an example one of the historical doctrines of a historical religion. In *Religion Within the Limits of Reason Alone* (p. 178) Kant declares that 'freedom is absolutely required' for the affirmation of every moral or religious belief, and it is clear that the requirement is a logical requirement. A man would not qualify as a believer in a particular moral or religious belief unless his assent to it was what theologians call an 'inner' assent. But the doctrine of the Resurrection, or of the Assumption of the Blessed Virgin Mary, or the story of the feeding of the five thousand, may be the object of a religious belief while still being understood in a sense in which it is unquestionably *either* true *or* false, quite independently of whether it is affirmed authentically or hypocritically or not at all.

These examples and descriptions may now serve as premises for some conclusions about the conflict between subjective and objective theories of ethics. They illustrate a difference between facts and values of the kind that subjective theorists make central in their arguments: a judgement of the quality of a salad involves and expresses the response of the person who judges it, and the involvement of the response in the judgement is so intimate that a discrepancy between the response and the ostensible content of the judgement requires us to question whether the speaker *means* what he says. When the statement he makes is that he has won a large sum of money, and he sounds unexpectedly gloomy about it, the discrepancy is external; however surprising his reaction may be, it does not have a similar bearing on the meaning of his claim.

It is natural and correct to express this contrast by saying that the expression of a feeling or attitude is part of the essence of the making of a value judgement, while it is not part of the essence of the making of a judgement about a plain matter of fact. The contrast deserves the attention that the subjectivist devotes to it, and that this way of expressing it invites for it. But in epistemological as in other descriptions it is necessary for the sake of completeness to make comparisons as well as contrasts. The subjectivist's account is intolerably partial because he is content with the contrast that he puts in the foreground of his picture. Some objective theorists may need reminding that the connection between a moral judgement and a feeling is more than merely external, but the reminder will go too far if it identifies the judgement with the expression of the feeling, so that no room is left for the consideration of the truth or falsehood of the content of the judgement. In the case of moral judgements, as in the case of religious affirmations, we need to be able to separate the question of the sincerity and integrity of the speaker, of the autonomy or authenticity of his judgement, from the further questions whether his judgement is justified or unjustified, sound or unsound, true or false. We may imagine an expert interrogator who acts as a consultant to the Inquisition and also to a godless dictatorship, discriminating the authentic from the inauthentic with unimpeachable fairness and accuracy, though himself indifferent to the subject matter of his questions and the truth or falsehood of his subjects' answers.

In isolating the peculiarity of a class of judgements we must beware of allowing it to obscure what that class has in common with other particular classes of judgements and what it has in common with all judgements as such. Philosophers are understandably but sometimes excessively preoccupied with the search for a *differentia*, and they may need to be reminded of forgotten similarities. An odd example from Lewis Carroll's *Through the Looking Glass* illustrates the need for the mutual support that comparison can give to contrast and contrast to comparison. Humpty Dumpty complains that all faces are the same – two eyes, a nose and a mouth, always arranged in the same pattern – so that we cannot be expected to distinguish one from another. Somebody who knew and recognised only what faces have in common, and could not distinguish one face from another, would be missing what is most important about faces for most purposes on most occasions. But somebody who knew only what was distinctive about each particular face, even if, which seems doubtful, he could be coherently envisaged and described, would be at least as much at a loss in dealing with ordinary questions and ordinary situations.

There are two analogous types of inadequacy that ethical theories may display. The more prevalent of the two is an excessive attention to what is distinctive about morality at the expense of the recognition of the wide area of overlap between the character of moral reasoning and the character of other modes of reasoning. Subjectivist, intuitionist, emotivist and prescriptivist theories are all guilty of various forms of this mistake. The other and less common mistake is made by some of the theories against which the authors of subjectivist paradoxes are reacting, and is liable to recur in accounts designed to answer the excesses of the sceptic. In his chapter on 'Scepticism in Ethics' in *The Concept of Philosophy* R. W. Newell writes (p. 123):

> It will be argued that there is no special problem about the justification of ethical statements. Of course there are problems specifically concerning ethical statements, namely the problems involved in deciding ethical issues in practice and supporting the decisions made; and these are no more philosophical problems than is the problem of supporting a political decision, or a scientific hypothesis, a problem for a philosopher rather than a politician or a scientist. But there is no *philosophical* problem of justification that is not equally a problem of the justification of an ethical judgement's traditional foil, judgements of fact. One main reason for the survival of ethical theories of the Humean genus is the belief in an illusory special puzzle. The mistake is to suppose that the difficulty of giving reasons for ethical statements is one *peculiar* to ethics, when it happens to be an inter-departmental difficulty shared by other, non-ethical statements as well.

This passage is instructive and striking because of the rarity of the mistake that it makes. Newell sees that the involvement of the emotions in moral disputes does not render them incapable of rational determination, any more than the frequent involvement of the emotions in disagreements about matters of fact puts them beyond the scope of evidence and argument. But in urging the truth and importance of this point that the sceptic misses he is led to overlook an important truth that the sceptic obscurely sees. There *is* a difference between the connection that human emotions have with questions of fact and the connection that human emotions have with questions of good and evil and right and wrong. The emotions are *directly* involved in moral judgements, as the sceptic claims or hints. They are involved in the meaning of moral judgements, and their connection with morality is not a matter of frequency or contingency, but a matter of logic or epistemology. But the sceptic is wrong to threaten, and Newell is wrong to fear, that an acknowledgement of the *a priori* connection between morality and the emotions will commit us to reducing moral judgements to expressions of emotion, taste or preference. Newell himself has shown elsewhere in his book a clear awareness that one feature or factor may be *a priori* connected with another without its being the case that the presence of either of them is either necessary or sufficient for the presence of the other. He has also explicitly recognised elsewhere that the interdepartmental difficulties – those puzzles about justification, reasons and criteria that recur in similar forms to threaten one by one the different kinds of human knowledge – are neither the only nor necessarily the most troublesome of the problems of philosophy. There are other and acute difficulties that arise from what distinguishes one species of knowledge from another. Newell illustrates in his accounts of scepticism about other minds and scepticism about material objects the role that the logical peculiarities of a kind of knowledge may play in a sceptical attack on it, and the contribution that such an attack may therefore make to the characterisation of the peculiarities. In moral philosophy, as in these other cases, scepticism can be answered only if we clearly distinguish the inter-departmental from the local difficulties and recognise that they call for separate treatment. Here as elsewhere it is only by misdescribing a logical peculiarity that one can enlist it in the cause of scepticism.

Newell is half right, and he is right about the part of the story that is usually the most seriously garbled. The sceptic to whom Newell is responding, and against whom he is over-reacting, is much less than half right. But he, like Newell, is led into error by the force of his attachment to something important that he is right about.

If we put together what we can learn from the sceptic and what we can learn from Newell, and try to separate it all from the mistakes by which it is encrusted, we find that in ethics, as in other fields of philosophy, there are both departmental difficulties and interdepartmental difficulties. Both kinds of difficulties must be resolved if we are to arrive at a just representation of the character of moral reasoning. The resolution of the interdepartmental problems is necessarily not the specific business of a book on a particular department of philosophy. But at least enough must be said about them to make sure that we have been able to isolate the departmental difficulties that are our specific preoccupation here. And there is a further reason why it is appropriate to continue to discuss non-moral judgements in a book specifically devoted to the characterisation of moral judgements: philosophical description, like any other form of description, proceeds by comparison and contrast, and in the description of morality we may and must use non-moral enquiries, judgements and disputes as objects of comparison and contrast with moral enquiries, judgements and disputes.

A good illustration of the soundness of these points of method can be provided by considering further a group of cases of non-moral judgements which we have seen to be significantly parallel to moral judgements in their logical structure, and hence also in the degree and nature of their vulnerability to sceptical criticism. They are one of the most discussed of all kinds of non-moral judgement, namely those that have to do with perception and the external world.

I call the perceptual cases a significantly parallel group because they too have given rise to forms of scepticism whose structural resemblance to moral scepticism matches the parallel between the features of the two kinds of judgements that have given rise to sceptical doubts. It is not for nothing that there have been 'moral sense' theories of ethics on the one hand, and on the other hand a tendency to scepticism about secondary qualities which bases itself on the fact that the reaction or response or experience of the speaker plays a crucial role in his verification of the claim that something is red or rancid. Both lines of thought originate from the recognition of an epistemological parallelism between sensory or perceptual judgements and evaluative judgements, and a corresponding awareness of some of the distinctions that may be drawn between those two groups of judgements taken jointly and many others.

Even here we are again beset by the danger, to which the ethical theorist nearly always succumbs, of making remarks designed to distinguish evaluative judgements from others and then finding that they apply to many judgements that are clearly not evaluative. Unless the parallel with perceptual judgements is used with great discretion, our description of evaluation will suffer from a form of this defect. For there is one feature that is strongly present both in perceptual and in evaluative judgements, and which is a source of many sceptical accounts of both kinds of judgements, but which is so far from being peculiar to these kinds that it is to be found in all kinds of judgement whatsoever. One way of expressing it is to make a somewhat paradoxical use of a platitudinous form of words: my reasons for any perceptual judgement that I make, and for any moral judgement that I make, and in general for *any* judgement that I make, must be *my* reasons. I cannot have any reason for affirming any proposition unless from what is referred to by that proposition there are unbroken lines of communication that terminate in something that is present or directly accessible to me here and now.

Few philosophers have failed to show awareness of this feature of enquiry, though such awareness has been characteristically obscure and distorted, expressed in forms of words that are liable, even when they are naturally capable of conveying an understanding of this feature, to convey also some other and mistaken or confusing impression that is also naturally expressed by these words in their familiar uses or in natural extensions of those uses. We have seen already that something can be learned from philosophical theories formulated in such a style. Here again we shall find that some attention to the confusing ways in which philosophers' general theories have misdescribed the nature of judgements is of direct assistance in the more laborious and less exciting task of offering an accurate point by point description.

The most extreme and unrestricted, but also the most picturesque and misleading form in which any philosopher has ever expressed an insight into this feature of enquiry is the thesis of the solipsist that his knowledge is always and necessarily knowledge of his own present sensations. William James was making the same point, and was nearer in his form of expression to the madness of solipsism than he would have been prepared to recognise, when he wrote his essay on 'The Sentiment of Rationality' (*The Will to Believe and Other Essays*, p. 63):

> What is the task which philosophers set themselves to perform; and why do they philosophize at all? Almost every one will immediately reply: They desire to attain a conception of the frame of things which shall on the whole be more rational than that somewhat chaotic view which every one by nature carries about with him under his hat. But suppose this rational conception attained, how is the philosopher to recognize it for what it is, and not let it slip through ignorance? The only answer can be that he will recognize its rationality as he recognizes everything else, by certain subjective marks with which it affects him. When he gets the marks, he may know that he has got the rationality.
>
> What, then, are the marks? A strong feeling of ease, peace, rest, is one of them. The transition from a state of puzzle and perplexity to rational comprehension is full of lively relief and pleasure.

C. I. Lewis perhaps reveals something of his pragmatist ancestry, but certainly shows a greater grip on sanity and common sense, when he gives us this more sober formulation (*An Analysis of Knowledge and Valuation*, p. 263):

> Ordinarily in citing the bases of what we say we know, we

not only let ourselves off with mention of proximate premises, taken for granted, but also we avail ourselves of any handy and pertinent information, whether from our own experience or from other sources. And the extent to which we learn from others is a distinctive feature marking the superiority of the human mentality. But obviously, what we thus learn must, in becoming knowledge for us, be credited; and credited by reference to grounds which are, eventually, those of first-person experience. It can have such credibility only by reference to our own past experience of receiving such reports and our subsequent experience of finding true or finding false what was reported. Receiving information from others and observing their behavior is – so experience has taught us – a relatively painless and a particularly fruitful mode of acquiring knowledge. But it is merely a complex way of learning from certain experiences of our own. And apart from a certain complexity which characterizes the interpretation of verbal signals, it is not particularly different from other ways of being advised of objective facts – not particularly different, for example, from learning by the reading of recording instruments. All knowledge is knowledge of someone; and ultimately no one can have any ground for his beliefs which does not lie within his own experience.

But Lewis has here, as sober philosophers will, sacrificed scope and even some sharpness of focus to sobriety of utterance. I shall therefore consider these three formulations in the descending order of comprehensiveness and caution in which I have set them down.

Wittgenstein said clearly, in one sentence of the *Tractatus Logico-Philosophicus*, what I shall now try to say equally clearly under the handicap of trying to say it in plain language and at greater length: 'What the solipsist means is, of course, correct.'

The point that the solipsist means to make is not restricted to any one type of judgement – perceptual, or psychological, or moral. He goes to the limit of declaring that he has no reason for believing in the existence or occurrence of anything but the present state of his own mind. When we set out the substance of his point in a less picturesque formulation, we need to preserve the wide scope of the solipsist's observations. What we have seen to be true of perceptual judgements and of moral judgements is expressible as a generalisation applicable to judgements of all kinds. It is in general true that if I make an unqualified assertion it is expected of me not only that I should have adequate grounds for the proposition that I assert, but also that those grounds should be of the most directly relevant kind. However strong my grounds may be, if they are to any degree indirect, if I have relied on testimony, authority, or circumstantial evidence, I am expected to give some notice of the character of my grounds, by the use of such phrases as 'I am told' or 'It is said' or 'there are some indications'.

As this last example shows, there are dangers of confusing the qualification by which I give notice of the indirectness of my grounds with another kind of qualification whose effect is to weaken an assertion or to make it more tentative. The confusion is easy to fall into because some of the idioms used for making qualifications of the one kind may also be used for making qualifications of the other kind. Here we need to distinguish, as often in philosophy, between two independent contrasts: (1) the contrast between one degree or strength of ground or reason and another, and (2) the contrast between one kind of ground or reason and another. It is when this distinction is not drawn that sceptical arguments can be made most plausible, and many sceptical theses and their grounds almost consist of a systematic failure to draw it. The future or the past is said to be unknowable because the occurrence of a past or future event necessarily cannot *now* be verified in the way appropriate to the verification of the occurrence of a present event. The dualist tells us that we cannot know what he is thinking because it is necessarily not open to us to be related as he is to the verification of statements about his mind. In all these cases the evidence that the sceptic condemns as indirect is, as he himself insists, necessarily the most direct evidence available at the time or to the person with whose verificational character or situation we are concerned. His scepticism is made plausible only by an unnoticed equivocation in his use of the terms 'direct' and 'indirect'. When he is in fact contrasting the most direct possible evidence for a proposition about a present event with the most direct possible evidence for a proposition about a past or future event he describes himself as contrasting direct evidence for a proposition about a present event with the indirectness of the only evidence available to somebody for whom that same event lies in the past or in the future. The contrast between my awareness of my own present states of mind and the necessarily different relation of a second or third person to any proposition about my present states of mind is likewise represented as a contrast between the direct evidence available to me and the merely indirect evidence available to you and others.

We may now see more clearly the significance for moral philosophy of the facts that I illustrated with the examples of the tossed salad and the play at the Haymarket. That the absence of a certain feeling of response on my part is a ground for doubting whether I *mean* what I say about the salad or the play is an indication that the response is a part of my justification for my remark, and that in the absence of the response I am not in the strongest possible position to make the remark that I do make. There is a clear analogy between these cases and the case of the blind man who says that his house has a red door. He cannot *ex hypothesi* be in the most directly favourable position for saying what he says; but he may nevertheless have adequate and even conclusive grounds for saying it. The absence of the most direct evidence or indications may be heavily outweighed by the presence of less direct indications, as when from my window at dusk I see no rain but see unfurled umbrellas.

Here again we need the distinction between a *kind* of reason, or authority, or justification, and a *degree* or *weight* or *strength* of evidence or argument. Such a distinction needs to be drawn wherever there is a contrast between what is directly and what is indirectly relevant to the truth of a conclusion. I may be justifiably certain that there is a fire in the grate, when all I have to go on is smoke from the chimney; that the tomato is ripe when I am blind or feeling it or eating it in the dark; that Napoleon lost the battle when I am a historian and not an eye witness; that the play at the Haymarket is amusing when I am reading the reviews and have not sat in the stalls.

When we say that the Duke of Wellington or the child with toothache or the man who had the dream or saw the play or the tomato knows in a way that we do not know, we must distinguish between two uses of these words: we may mean that the Duke or the child or the man does know something that we do not know, or we may mean that his *way* of knowing is different from ours. The truth of the remark in the second interpretation is not even a good reason for supposing it to be true in the first. Norman Malcolm's suspicion of the conclusions liable to be drawn from research into correlations between dream reports and rapid eye movements, like his insistence in his other work on the philosophy of mind that a person is authoritative in the answers that he gives to questions about his own present states of mind ('His answer is *the* answer'), is a natural expression of respect for the special character of a *kind* of evidence; but it is disguised as a suggestion, as misleading as it is persuasive, that the dreamer or the sufferer knows something that cannot be known by another with the same degree of assurance. The dualist, Cartesian, sound of this part of Malcolm's story might have been a warning to him that he was falling into old traps, just as Wittgenstein ought to have drawn back – unless he was being deliberately

provocative – from answering the paradoxes of Descartes
with counter-paradoxes that simply stand them on their
heads: 'I can know what someone else is thinking, not what I
am thinking. It is correct to say "I know what you are
thinking" and wrong to say "I know what I am thinking" '
(*Philosophical Investigations*, p. 222).

Paradoxes like these are strange instruments to find in the
toolbox of a philosopher who professes to be aiming only at
a description of the workings of our language, and the use of
them is certainly at odds with some of Wittgenstein's own
pronouncements on his task and its methods. Yet they serve
his purpose: by them we are helped to see the character of
minds and the ways of speaking that are appropriate to
them. Other sources of help available to us in pursuing the
same enterprise are the paradoxes of traditional dualism and
scepticism against which Wittgenstein was protesting, and
the point-by-point description which he sometimes offered
as well as promised. A misdescription is a partial description, and a sceptical or metaphysical paradox by its
misdescription contributes to the characterisation of what it
also misrepresents. It is therefore appropriate to invoke in
the course of trying to describe morality not only the
examples with which we began, but also the ethical
'theories' that Newell was concerned to correct, and the still
wider theories of James and Lewis and the author of the
Tractatus that we have been able to bring to bear on the dual
process of describing the place of reason and feeling in
morality; a dual process in that it consists of showing both
how morality resembles and how morality differs from what
is not morality.

In morality, as in psychology, we are concerned with the
subjective reactions of individuals and at the same time with
a subject matter that calls for and permits all that those
philosophers have usually had in mind who have defended
the concept of moral objectivity.

CHAPTER 5

OBJECTIVITY

I have tried to refute subjectivism about ethics without denying the essential involvement of feelings and emotions in moral judgement and moral reasoning, and hence without denying the essential involvement in ethics of something that can properly be described as subjective. In my exposition and argument I have made free use of the terms 'subjective' and 'objective' and their correlates, but I have not so far given any account of their various senses or uses. Like most writers on ethics, I have treated them as if they are clearer than they are, and in particular I have omitted to note explicitly how variously they are used in different contexts, and even in different ethical contexts. I have not even distinguished between the ordinary uses of the words and the special and technical uses to which they have been put by some philosophers.

His recognition of this sort of difficulty, and a certain impatience with the tendency of philosophers to ride rough-shod over it, have prompted Hare to say, in his article 'The Objectivity of Values' (*Common Factor*, June 1964) and on numerous other occasions, that the controversy between subjective and objective theories of ethics is radically misconceived. He suggests that the meaning of the terms 'subjectivist' and 'objectivist' is now so uncertain that the terms should in future be reserved for use in historical studies of ethical philosophy before 1935.

Even if Hare were right about the philosophical uses of these terms, there would remain some valuable ordinary uses of the words 'subjective' and 'objective', and Hare would presumably not wish to deny this. When we look at some of these uses we find some indications that Hare is wrong to urge us to banish these and related words from substantive discussion of problems in philosophical ethics. A father's judgement of the intelligence or good looks of his own child, or an enthusiast's estimate of the chances of his own football club or racehorse, is often and reasonably dismissed as 'subjective'. A doctor does not normally treat the members of his immediate family, or a professor examine his own children in the Tripos. These tasks are assigned to others who may be expected to take a more 'objective' view. It is clear that in these and comparable cases the contrast between a more and a less subjective judgement can be drawn only because the judgements are concerned with questions to which it is possible to find answers that are independent of the prejudices and predilections of those who make the judgements.

Some specially clear illustrations of this point are to be found among cases involving quantity and measurement. It can be said in a court of law that the witnesses' conflicting estimates of the speed of a vehicle are 'subjective' only because it is understood and agreed that the question whether a car was travelling at or above or below 40 m.p.h. is an objectively determinable question to which bystanders who are not equipped with the appropriate instruments, especially if they are also interested parties, notoriously give unreliable and conflicting answers. Two drivers whose cars collide will usually give conflicting answers even when they were provided with speedometers.

It is equally notorious that a man's moral judgements are liable to be prejudiced in his own favour and in favour of his kith and kin. Nepotism is an eponymous but not the only species of injustice prompted by family loyalty and affection.

But these facts are not fitted for the use that sceptics try to make of them. A man cannot be shown to have made a mistake in his own favour unless he can be shown to have made a mistake. A sceptic who refers to this kind of subjectivity in moral choice and judgement is therefore defeating himself as a sceptic always does when he uses the fact that we now *know* a judgement of a particular kind to be mistaken as a ground for the conclusion that judgements of that kind cannot in principle be known to be true or to be false.

Newell's suggestion that there is no special problem about the justification of moral judgements arises from his recognition of the importance in moral conflicts of the species of subjectivity that I have just referred to, and it deserves most of the emphasis that he implicitly gives to it. Since I may so easily make mistakes of fact or logic in my own favour when my interests are closely bound up with the answer to a question, it is not surprising that in moral disputes, in which, on any view of their logical character, the interests and emotions of the disputants are always or usually involved, it should be common for the parties to be partial, to betray that their grasp of the issues is both incomplete and distorted by prejudice.

There is another sense of subjectivity in which we may recognise that there is an element of subjectivity in typical moral judgements without compromising the objectivity that I have been defending. The word 'subjective' may be used to mark the presence of the logical feature that Wisdom calls 'verificational asymmetry,' which is specially charac-teristic of propositions about minds. Every proposition about a state of mind is such that the verificational relation of one person to that proposition is necessarily dif-ferent from that of any other person. The person who is specially placed is the person whose state of mind is in question. When he makes a remark about his own state of mind he is the subject of his remark both in the sense that the remark is about him and that he himself makes the remark. The former sense happens to be one that may also be naturally and correctly expressed by saying that he is the object of the remark, and if we do express it in that way, while expressing the latter sense by 'subject', we are contrasting subject and object in the way that leads us to speak of the world of objects or of objective fact in contrast to man as subject or to a subjective world of feeling and experience.

None of this has any tendency to undermine the rational, interpersonal, and in that sense objective, determinability of questions and disputes about human feelings and experiences. Whether somebody feels sick or hates the Pope or does like to be beside the seaside is a matter of fact, and if we call it 'subjective', and mean by that that it is about a person and not about an inanimate object, we must not be misled into thinking that we have given any reason for thinking that its truth value is in any way or to any degree dependent on what anybody believes or wishes it to be.

The words 'subjective' and 'objective' have one use in which moral judgements are rightly called subjective, though to recognise this is not to make any concession to the subjectivist or sceptic. The sense I have in mind is exemplified in the phrase 'objective test' when it is used to apply to a 'multiple choice' examination or to any similarly mechanical procedure of grading. This is akin to, though distinguishable from, the sense in which an estimate of the speed of a car is subjective if it is made without the use of a speedometer or other instrumental means. The examiner of an essay may say 'I gave him (or it) 58' or 'I think it deserves B—.' The marker of an objective test will say instead 'He scored 90'. There is no scope or need in such a test for judgement by the examiner, and hence no place in his declaration of the result for a reference to himself and his view of the work. But it does not follow that in the case of the essay that cannot in this sense be 'objectively' marked there is no interpersonal standard of merit to be applied, that all judgements are 'subjective' in the sense that any view is as good as any other. It is true and notorious that examiners differ in the marking of essays, and that essay marks are therefore an unreliable guide to merit, but as in the case of the speeds of vehicles there could not be any meaning in the complaint of unreliability except on the assumption that there are rights and wrongs in judgements of the relevant species.

One of the 'interdepartmental' factors of scepticism which nevertheless operates with special force in the case of moral scepticism, is illustrated as clearly as anywhere in this short passage from a paper of mine on 'Plato's Political Analogies' (p. 114):

> There is nothing to which my decision must correspond in order to be a reasonable decision in the way that my belief must correspond to what the world is like in order to be a true belief; and so there is nothing to prevent your decision and my decision from both being reasonable although your decision is different from mine.

These words were written under the malign influence of the idea that objectivity requires an object. When I wrote them I had no answer to the question that I should now wish to put to any philosopher who wrote the same words now: 'Is there anything in the world that a logical or mathematical remark must correspond to in order to be a true remark?' The idea that all truth is correspondence is first cousin to the idea that the meaning of a word is an object.

The misleading effects of these ideas are not confined to the philosophy of logic and moral philosophy. They touch even the modes of knowledge that they use as paradigms against what they represent as oblique or deviant modes. But ethics and logic depart most evidently from those paradigms, and hence these misunderstandings affect them more directly and persuasively, with the result that sceptics and their readers may overlook both the applicability of the same sceptical considerations to physics and to ordinary perceptual judgements, and therefore the kinship in logical character on which it is founded.

The picture of a 'world of absolute values' is drawn with the freest hand by those who combine the idea that objectivity requires an object with the idea that to make a moral judgement is necessarily to invoke or to purport to invoke an unexceptionable moral rule or principle. Those who retain the second of these ideas after they have rightly rejected the first will be prompted, like Hare and Braithwaite, to represent moral reasoning as the deductive derivation of particular judgements from universal principles which have been adopted without any reasons at all.

At this point a number of philosophical paths come together from various directions.

To follow the first path that opens before us is to try to be clear about the relation between questions of fact and logic on the one hand, and questions of morality on the other. I have just been contrasting morality with matters of fact and matters of logic almost as the sceptic does, and in numerous places where I was concerned to answer his objections I have come near to accepting at least the terms in which they were expressed. But the view towards which I am finally reaching involves me in narrowing if not obliterating the contrast of which the sceptic makes so much. I do not of course deny that there are logical questions which are not moral questions, or that there are factual questions which are not moral questions. But I do deny that there are any moral questions which are not also questions of fact or questions of logic or mixtures of questions of fact and questions of logic.

I can best make my meaning plain by a further reference to Hume's remark that after every circumstance and every relation is known the reason has no further room to operate. Hume was right to hold that if every question of logic and every question of fact had been answered there could remain no question calling for the use of the reason, but he was wrong to imply, if he did, like some of his followers, imply it, that there could still remain a moral question, which could accordingly call only for the operation of the passions and the sentiments. There can be a difference of feeling or reaction, unmixed with any dispute as to a matter of fact or a matter of logic, and such a difference may legitimately be called a disagreement, but it cannot properly be called a *moral* disagreement if that is all it amounts to.

Hume thought not only that it was abstractly possible but also that it frequently happened that two men were in dispute about a moral question when no question of fact or of logic was at issue between them, and in this too he has been followed by his modern disciples. But neither Hume nor any of his disciples has ever produced an example of a moral dispute in which nothing divides the parties except a difference of feeling that persists after all the relevant facts are in and all the relevant points of logic are settled. I do not believe that it is even theoretically possible that such an instance should occur, and I believe still less that such instances occur with the frequency which is alleged by moral sceptics.

The position can be clarified by examining the concepts of 'circumstance' and 'relation', or matter of fact and matter of logic. It is in their misconceptions about these ideas that we can find the sources of the misrepresentations by Hume and his party of the character of moral disagreement. When they say that all the facts are in they mean that no question about what is to be expected in the future now divides the disputants. When they say that 'every relation is known', or that all the relevant points of logic are settled, they mean that the parties no longer disagree on any point on which a settlement could be reached by a deductive or formal procedure. But from the fact that two people do not disagree about any question calling for further observation or experiment it does not follow that they do not disagree about any question of fact; and two people may disagree about a question of logic without disagreeing about any question that could be answered by a purely formal procedure.

But the correction of mistakes about the scope and nature of factual disagreement and logical disagreement is not sufficient to guard against the danger of seeing moral disagreement as a head-on conflict of feelings or choices or arbitrarily chosen principles or unreasoned intuitions. Another familiar factor is at work: the idea that what is logical or factual is not moral, and must be set aside when we seek a characterisation of moral judgements and conflicts (see Chapter 2, pp. 24–5). However wide we make our understanding of factual and logical enquiry we shall not recognise the objectivity of moral enquiry if we exclude from it everything that is factual and logical. The effect of such an exclusion will naturally be to make us see the essence of the moral where the sceptic sees it, in the sheer clash of the arbitrary against the arbitrary.

Hare and Braithwaite both anticipate and both try to answer the charge that they represent the choice of ultimate moral principles as arbitrary and unreasoned. In his section on 'Decisions of Principle' in *The Language of Morals*, Hare writes (p. 69):

if pressed to justify a decision completely, we have to give a complete specification of the way of life of which it is a part. This complete specification it is impossible in practice to give; the nearest attempts are those given by the great religions, especially those which can point to historical persons who carried out the way of life in practice. Suppose, however, that we can give it. If the inquirer still goes on asking 'But why *should* I live like that?' then there is no further answer to give him, because we have already, *ex hypothesi*, said everything that could be included in this further answer. We can only ask him to make up his own

mind which way he ought to live; for in the end everything
rests upon such a decision of principle. He has to decide
whether to accept that way of life or not; if he accepts it, then
we can proceed to justify the decisions that are based upon
it; if he does not accept it, then let him accept some other,
and try to live by it.

Hare recognises that it is at this point that his critic will
accuse him of resting moral judgements on ultimately
arbitrary choices, and he defends himself by offering a
supposedly parallel case (ibid.):

> To describe such ultimate decisions as arbitrary, because *ex
> hypothesi* everything which could be used to justify them has
> already been included in the decision, would be like saying
> that a complete description of the universe was utterly
> unfounded, because no further fact could be called upon in
> corroboration of it. This is not how we use the words
> 'arbitrary' and 'unfounded'. Far from being arbitrary, such
> a decision would be the most well-founded of decisions,
> because it would be based upon a consideration of
> everything upon which it could possibly be founded.

Braithwaite quotes and endorses these remarks in his
Eddington Lecture (*An Empiricist's View of the Nature of Religious
Belief*, p. 34), and adds a sentence from the last page of
Nowell-Smith's *Ethics*: 'The questions "What shall I do?"
and "What moral principles should I adopt?" must be
answered by each man for himself; that at least is part of the
connotation of the word "moral".'

Hare's parallel with a total description of the universe is a
hostage offered to his critics. If there were such a thing as a
complete description it could not of course be extended or
further corroborated, but it could certainly be examined for
its adequacy to the phenomena and states of affairs that it
purported to describe. And it is certain that if you and I offer
alternative 'total descriptions', and they really are rivals and
not just alternative formulations of the same content, then

there is a conflict between us such that at most one of us has given a correct total description, and it will be for investigation and reflection to determine which if either of us has given such a correct description. A correct description, whether total or partial, is 'founded' on an examination of what it describes.

For Hare seriously to intend the parallel as an account of ultimate ethical choice and judgement would be for him to withdraw nearly everything else that he says both in *The Language of Morals* and in *Freedom and Reason*. According to his often reiterated account, there can be alternative systems or sets of ultimate principles, and it is possible for you to choose one set and me to choose another without its being the case that either of us is wrong in his choice. That our principles conflict is a fact that has to be accepted as beyond the influence of argument. In that case, however carefully and fully you and I have taken into account everything that could possibly be relevant to our moral choices, it is hard to see that we could in any sense be said to 'found' or 'base' our decisions on such a consideration or on anything at all. Hare would be more faithful to his own usual theory if he forswore the parallel with propositions of fact and acknowledged that on his view our ultimate moral decisions are arbitrary reactions or responses *to* the universe. A response is not founded or based on that to which it is a response unless it satisfies just the sorts of conditions that according to Hare are not satisfied by ultimate moral judgements.

On the next page of the *Language of Morals* (p. 70) we find Hare again appealing to 'an interesting analogy with the position of the scientist.' He refers to Kant's remarks on the Autonomy of the Will (Kant, *The Moral Law*, p. 88), and reaffirms that each of us must make his own decisions of principle. But this time instead of contrasting ethics and science as he does when speaking in *Freedom and Reason* of our freedom to adopt our own moral principles, he points out that a scientist must analogously rely on his own observations, and can learn to trust the observations of others only by checking them in the first instance against his own.

Hare's aim is to reconcile the rationality of moral argument with his thesis that we are free to adopt our fundamental moral principles. But when he says that we are free to form our moral opinions in a stronger sense than that in which we are free to form our opinions about the facts he is not so much distinguishing as confusing two kinds of freedom. The progress of science, which is an objective, rational progress, not only allows but requires, as Mill and others have insisted, complete freedom *of enquiry*, freedom from external authorities and constraints. The scientific enquirer demands freedom of opinion and expression, but he remains subservient to the force and authority of evidence and argument. Moral enquiry and moral judgement rightly demand the same freedom but are rightly subject to the same coercion.

The authenticity of moral response that Sartre and other Existentialists insist upon is connected with this sense of freedom. Sartre declares that we are free and must 'invent' our morality. Sartre differs from Hare in that he altogether dispenses with rationality in ethics, on the assumption that to bow to the force of argument would be to submit to a tyranny that would trammel the agent's freedom and destroy the authenticity of his choices. But Hare and Sartre agree in leaving us free to adopt, choose, invent our fundamental moral positions without any constraint such as they believe would be imposed by recognising that there can be reasoning *de finibus bonorum et malorum*.

I quote Hare and Sartre as typical and prominent examples of contemporary analytical and existentialist philosophers of morals who are 'moral sceptics' in my sense of the phrase, in that they do not recognise the existence or the possibility of such a thing as moral knowledge. But it is important to my purpose to emphasise that they *are* typical. Many other thinkers of both groups have put forward, explicitly or by implication, similar accounts of moral enquiry. The *acte gratuit* of Gide is gratuitous in the sense that there is no *reason* for it, and it is held to achieve its total authenticity only *by* being unreasoned. If it were not wholly arbitrary it would not be wholly free. Professor Bernard Williams questions what he calls 'ethical realism': ethical discourse is 'discourse which the world has to fit' and not 'discourse which has to fit the world' (*Problems of the Self*, p. 203).

I suggest that these accounts, both analytical and existentialist, are characteristic philosophical theories about ethical reasoning and knowledge: characteristic both in their distortions of the nature of such reasoning and knowledge, and in the plausibility that they derive from the fact that they are not *mere* distortions. They caricature and parody, misrepresent and exaggerate, features that genuinely do belong to moral knowledge and enquiry, and the distortions are characteristically difficult to correct because a plain denial of any of the paradoxical and distorted accounts is itself liable to issue in a rival paradox, to convey another distorted impression. Once again we see that every tempting philosophical formula or form of words is capable either of conveying something true or of conveying something false about the logical character of the reasoning or knowledge that it refers to. Only a neutral description will save us from an endless conflict between rival theories each of which is partly true and partly false, and each of which mistakenly agrees with the others in supposing that one and only one such theory is wholly true.

These mistaken ethical theories have an even closer link with other philosophical theories. They largely arise from and express a set of misunderstandings that recur repeatedly in considering other philosophical and epistemological problems. Largely, but not wholly: and the importance and nature of this qualification can best be explained by making a few further brief remarks about philosophical disputes in general and then reconsidering in more detail the special case of disputes about the objectivity of morals.

CHAPTER 6

CONFLICT

When we have seen that sceptical and subjective theories of ethics are prompted by distorted apprehension of features that actually belong to ethical judgements and disputes, we have seen not only that such theories are false but also that they contain important elements of truth. A caricature misleads us if we take it to be a photographic portrait, but it may enlighten us if we recognise that it is a caricature. Wittgenstein dismissed philosophical theorising because philosophical theories are all false. If we endorse his conclusion as well as his premise we shall miss valuable opportunities of making use of the theories in the furthering of the enterprise, in which Wittgenstein himself was primarily interested, of describing what the theories were meant to describe. For one thing, the theories evidently and notoriously conflict with each other, and this means that we can often learn from one of them to correct the distortions committed by another. But it is also true that one theory will often be found to agree with another on points as fundamental as those on which the theories mutually disagree, and this fact has a dual importance for the task of positive description. In some cases we can learn part of what we need to know, show part of what we need to show, by denying something erroneous that is agreed between two conflicting theories. In such cases we can often account for and resolve the conflict by identifying a common error whose exposure reveals that there are positive and correct points in each of the theories which are accordingly compatible with positive and correct points in the other, though the compatibility was hidden by the common confusion. But secondly – and this is a point of at least equal value to the aspirant after a non-theoretical, 'aseptic', description – two or more theories may agree on *truths* as important as any falsehoods on which they agree, and as important as any truths or falsehoods on which they disagree. If we are prepared to exploit these facts about theories we can hope to combine the detailed accuracy for whose sake Wittgenstein abandoned theories with the perspective and scope and generality that the theorists are seeking.

If we pursue this policy we soon discover how striking is the agreement on the fundamental character of morality that underlies the forest of disagreements both about some of its subordinate features and about how its main features are to be summarily described. And once we have perceived this we can harness the efforts of our predecessors in moral philosophy to our task of description, and can then see how relatively trivial is the residual conflict about the choice of a label or title or frame for the finished picture.

Nowell-Smith sums up what he takes to be the upshot of his whole book, *Ethics*, when he says on p. 320 that in ethics every man must answer for himself; and in the spirit of the rest of his work he regards this as a point of contrast between ethics and other modes of enquiry. Sartre is making substantially the same point in *Existentialism and Humanism* when he says that 'man is condemned at every instant to invent man'; there is no human nature antecedent to man's choices, and they are and must be the choices of the individual man. Hare calls his second book *Freedom and Reason* because his purpose is to reconcile with the rationality of ethical enquiry what he sees as its pre-eminent autonomy: he says that we must be free to form our opinions on moral questions in some sense in which we are not free to form our opinions on matters of fact and matters of logic. The contrast is here explicit, and again the stress is on the individuality and autonomy of the response that is required of the moral agent and the moral judge. Margaret Macdonald, in her essay 'Ethics and the Ceremonial Use of Language' in Max Black's collection *Philosophical Analysis*, says that 'in ethics we can never go to sleep' as if she supposed that in some other modes of rational enquiry we might be allowed on occasion to relax our vigilance. The emphasis is again on the need for a first-hand, authentic response. Either there are no rules, or there are rules that I must re-enact for myself; I must internalise them as *my* policies and externalise them as *my* practices.

This last way of speaking is at once reminiscent of the language used by other philosophers whose entrenchments are ordinarily thought to be drawn up against those of Hare and Hume, Braithwaite and Nowell-Smith. Bishop Butler is preaching on the text that makes man 'a law unto himself' when he says that the transgressor is self-condemned: the law by which he is judged is a law that he has himself subscribed to. In another place he suggests that we can find out the truths of morals by remarking what every man 'puts on the show of'. When a man is defending his own conduct, or appraising that of others, he shows his recognition of the relevance of principles and standards of assessment by which his own actions may need to be severely judged. He shows his understanding of what is right and wrong, good and bad; and it is a shared understanding, since it is a show that *all* men put on. That is why it is possible, when a man departs from what is recognised to be good conduct, to convict him of irrationality, of inconsistency, of contradicting *himself*, of denying something in his own mind and character, and not just flouting some external authority or resisting some external force. Kant is giving expression in a different idiom to the same understanding when he speaks of the moral agent and judge as a legislator, enacting the moral law for himself, willing only what he can consistently require of all rational beings as such. The fact that Kant is concerned to underline *both* the need for autonomy that is attested by all these witnesses, *and* the compatibility of that autonomy with the objectivity and rationality of the law, strikingly illustrates how much ethical theorists can differ on other and fundamental points while still sharing their recognition of what we have seen to be the central feature of moral action and judgement: its authenticity and individuality: the fact that it is or enacts the judgement of the person himself at first hand. This recognition crosses even the gulf that is fixed between objective theorists and extreme subjectivists.

The list could be extended further, and each addition would strengthen rather than qualify the main conclusion. Prichard and Moore and Ewing and Ross, when they defended their different forms of intuitionism, were representing moral insight as a kind of *seeing*, and so insisting in their styles, different from each other and from those of Hare and Kant and Butler and Sartre, that the moral truth must be presented to *my* eyes, must be accessible authentically to *me*, if it is to guide and govern my conduct or to illuminate my judgement of men and motives, actions and events. The same structure is found in 'moral sense' theories, according to which moral perception is again analogous to sense-perception. The eye of the mind, like any other eye, may be darkened by blindness or impeded by obstacles that occlude what it is trying to see. The eye is fitted and equipped for its purpose only if it has good sight and its objects are unveiled before it. To know the truth only by hearsay or on authority is to be like the blind man who knows that the books are red or that the tomatoes are ripe but who does not see for himself that they are red or ripe.

The characterisation of moral disagreement that begins to emerge from this survey is nowhere more fully and clearly elaborated than in the Socratic dialogues of Plato. In the

Gorgias, Socrates is not content to enlist the agreement of the bystanders against Polus or Callicles. He is determined to show that his opponent is contradicting himself as well as Socrates. When he says to him 'You yourself will be found to disagree with what you have been saying', the prediction that Callicles can be brought by argument to admit something incompatible with his declared position is at the same time a comment on his present state of mind and state of heart. The allegation is that his mind is confused and that his feelings are in mutual disharmony. The same picture is painted with stronger lines and in brighter colours in Books VIII and IX of the *Republic*, where the portrait of the tyrannical man represents him as unhappy because of the warring desires within his soul as well as ignorant and muddled because of the mutually hostile beliefs in his disordered mind. There is an adumbration here of Aristotle's unification of desire and reason in action and choice, though in Plato's picture the two elements are seen as parallel rather than as merged in a single act or state. In both accounts it is recognised that a moral conflict, whether between two or more human beings or between warring elements in a single soul, involves both the understanding and the emotions, so that its resolution can be achieved only by a combination of rational reflection and psychological integration. The purpose of these changes is to extrude false ideas and wrong purposes so that the recognition of truth will be accompanied by a settled disposition to feel and act in the ways that right reason directs.

The myth of the *Phaedrus* gives a formal metaphysical dress to the same conception of moral perplexity and disagreement. Plato declares that every human soul *tetheatai ta onta* – has seen the eternal Forms. No soul is allowed to transmigrate into a human body unless it has been granted a moral and intellectual vision sufficient to ensure that it knows the most fundamental of the truths on which Plato wishes to insist. It follows that a soul in which false beliefs take root is a soul in conflict with itself; the ignorant or wicked man is denying the truth that is in him, and is therefore guilty of *self*-contradiction in a sense stronger than any that we normally give to that expression.

The description of morality to which these thinkers all contribute is a correct description, as can best be shown by a direct examination of the nature of moral disagreement, freed as far as possible from the special terms and categories used by the particular philosophers I have quoted.

In ethics, Broad said, all we can do is 'to twit each other with inconsistency'. The implication is that moral argument lacks foundations such as are thought to be supplied in scientific investigation by experience and experiment, in mathematics by axioms and postulates, in law by statutes or authoritatively settled cases. Hence, it is thought, we can never establish or refute a moral judgement, but at best only demonstrate that two judgements conflict, and that one or other of them will have to be given up. If a man's moral views are mutually consistent, they can never be convicted of irrationality. 'After every circumstance, every relation is known, the understanding has no further room to operate, nor any object on which it could employ itself.' If at that stage you and I still disagree, our difference is to be attributed to the passions and the sentiments. If we agree, it is because we *feel* similarly towards the objects on which, up to that point, our understanding had been employing itself. And if men in general react in roughly or closely similar ways, that is just a fact about the fabric and constitution of the human species, and has no force as a justification of the shared reactions, or as an objection to the divergent reactions of a Thrasymachus or a Hitler, a Polus or a Genghis Khan. Plato is simply being dogmatic when he claims that all men react in fundamentally similar ways, and is being even more dogmatic when he chooses to describe as 'the truth' the standpoint from which all or most men do react in the last resort. It is simply our good fortune that most of us share our chief human sentiments, and the ease with which we can imagine beings who differ from us fundamentally in this respect seems to show that community of response is no ground for the establishment of the validity of the content or tendency of the common responses.

An important part of the reply that this line of argument needs can be given even if we accept the terms in which it is conducted and even before we question the basis of the supposed contrast between moral and non-moral enquiries. If we found that we were unable to answer sceptical arguments based on the suppositions about disagreement that the sceptic brings against us, the practical upshot of the discussion would not be greatly altered. The extremes of mutual unintelligibility that we are called upon to consider are imaginary extremes, and even if they did not prove to be incoherent suppositions they would remain as little more than remote objects of comparison with our ordinary experience. We never do, and in real life never could, meet somebody with whom we have nothing in common. In real life we discuss questions only with human beings, and there are no human beings with whom we have nothing in common, even if it had been possible to allow that there conceivably might have been.

But there is no need to make use of this interim reply to the line of argument that begins with Broad's dictum. The supposed contrast between moral and non-moral enquiries cannot be made out, and the argument accordingly fails more fundamentally. Even in mathematics and physics the possibility of presenting argument and evidence depends on shared responses between the parties to a disagreement. The fabric and constitution of the human species includes the fabric and constitution of the human understanding. Even Hume's own word 'sentiments' helps by its etymology to break down the contrast that some of his remarks imply. *Sentire* is to opine as well as to feel: my sentiments include my *sententiae* or judgements as well as my feelings in the

narrower sense. And it is because we share the same faculties
of sense and understanding that we can reason together
about questions of fact and questions of logic. We are
making remarks that belong to what Wittgenstein
appropriately called the 'natural history' of the human
species if we note that human beings typically respond in
these ways rather than in those, whether the responses are
those that constitute what Hume calls the sentiment of
humanity or those that Wittgenstein himself presents as the
common ground on which we build our understanding.

The observations of philosophical natural history may be
reinforced by an abstract argument whose upshot for the
concepts of reason and objectivity, whether in ethics of
elsewhere, is to the same effect. It is a fact of natural history
that members of the human species share certain faculties or
dispositions or powers of reasoning. But it is not a fact of
natural history, or a natural fact of any other kind, that the
sharing of some such powers or responses is necessary for the
conduct of enquiry and dispute. The necessity in question is
not causal but logical: nothing can qualify as *communication* –
here again the etymology is helpful – unless it is a transaction
between beings who share a common understanding. This
can be shown by an argument that makes no reference to
the special features of any particular mode or modes of
enquiry: (1) you and I cannot be known to be in conflict
unless it is possible to identify a proposition that I assert with
a proposition that you deny; (2) no such proposition can be
identified unless there is some expression that you and I use
in the same way; (3) if we use an expression in the same way
then we regard the same steps as relevant to determining the
truth or falsehood of what is expressed by it; for a
disagreement about what *is* relevant is or involves a
disagreement about what the dispute is that we are engaged
in, and when such a case of cross-purposes is resolved it
resolves itself either into agreement or into a disagreement
to which all these conditions again apply.

This argument is sufficiently abstract to apply without distinction to moral and non-moral communication and dispute, and this is just as we should expect from our more informal observations of the structure of enquiry. If we did not respond similarly to similar situations, then we could not communicate either about morality or about anything else. The whole of epistemology, and not just the epistemology of morals, needs to give a central place to this community of reaction and response. If anything needs or deserves to be recognised as the 'foundation' of knowledge and understanding it is this community and the acquisition of the powers of speech and thought that it makes possible.

We are now arrived at a plainer if not clearer formulation of the truth that Plato expresses in the *Phaedrus* myth. It is true that every human being shares some of his knowledge and understanding with every other human being, and hence that whenever one man denies what another man asserts at least one of them will be found on full enquiry to have committed himself to a position that he cannot reasonably combine with his initial assertion. This is why the terms and conditions of Socratic dialectic are so natural and effective as means for the conduct of collaborative or competitive reflection, and why it could be said that competitive reflection is itself a species of collaborative reflection. Each party judges his opponent's submissions by reference to what his opponent must admit because it is part of the common stock of knowledge or understanding. Sceptics accordingly recognise that in order to produce persuasive cases of dramatic deadlock they must invent beings whose reactions differ deeply from those of the human beings that we know. The extremes of mutual unintelligibility that we are called upon to consider are imaginary extremes, and even if they had not been shown by abstract argument to be incoherent suppositions, they would remain as little more than remote objects of comparison with our ordinary experience. Before we reach the ideal limit of irresoluble disagreement we have passed into mutual incomprehension. If the Martian or the Brobdingnagian is *too* different from us in his opinions and reactions, we have to say that we do not understand him. In real life we discuss questions only with human beings, and there are no human beings with whom we have nothing in common. It has not even proved possible to allow that there conceivably might have been.

With the human beings that we meet, whether in co-operation or in conflict, we find and shall continue to find that by relying on what we have in common we can engage in debate in which the area of common ground can be extended. Sometimes we reach deadlock, but we never reach a *necessary* deadlock. Often we come to the end of our powers or our patience, but never to a point at which nothing more *could* be said.

In describing the progress and conduct of moral disputes philosophers have characteristically overlaid some accurate observations with misrepresentations arising from their theoretical prejudices. When Broad said that in ethics we can do no more than 'twit each other with inconsistency' he was probably supposing that the distinction he drew between ethics and other enquiries was greater than it is; but by this phrase he did happily hit off what we actually do in moral disagreements. Hare explicitly holds what Broad hints at: that the need for a shared starting point defeats the hope or fear of providing in ethical disputes what is held to be available elsewhere, and to be necessary for fully rational enquiry: starting points or first principles which are either self-evident or in some other way enforceable on an opponent on pain of irrationality. But he too gives a good description of the customary processes of moral debate. Further contributions can be gathered from numerous philosophers whose theories differ widely among themselves and from those of Broad and Hare: Hume, Prichard, Rashdall, Moore, Ross and Stevenson.

All these theorists, while differing on points of sometimes important detail, agree on the outline of a description of moral disputation according to which what is central in it is the challenge 'What about ...?' or 'Suppose *you* were in that situation ...' or 'How would it be if everybody ...?' or some other of the many forms of the challenge to be consistent. Now it is abstractly plausible to say that two conflicting 'systems of values' might be mutually independent and individually comprehensive, so that, as in the case of the two total pictures of the universe invoked in the correspondingly unrealistic argument against coherence theories of truth, there is nothing to choose between them and no hope of reconciling them. But in both instances our actual situation is different and inescapably different from the sceptic's blueprint. We remain burdened with the 'immense mass of cognition' of which Peirce speaks in his Critique of Berkeley's Idealism. What I believe and know, however much I may be at loggerheads with you, includes some of what you know and believe, and it is not therefore open to us to pursue our disagreement to the sceptic's imagined limit without settling it: at least one of us will contradict himself in the end by contradicting what both of us know or believe.

The suggestion that an effective critical argument will typically involve showing that an opponent must choose between two mutually inconsistent theses may appear to involve the paradoxical implication that all falsehoods are contradictions, and so to take us back to unfashionable metaphysical theories like the coherence theory of truth, and Spinoza's view that the order and connection of ideas is the same as the order and connection of things, and Leibniz's principle of sufficient reason. A fuller explanation will show that my account does not lead to such dramatic consequences, but will at the same time make clear that these views, and in particular the coherence theory of truth, express or imply important truths whose truth or importance is disguised from many philosophers by the traditional costumes in which they are often dressed.

The role of contradiction, and hence of logic in a very strict sense of the word, is central to enquiry and dispute in general, even when its subject matter is empirical or moral and not itself logical in that strict sense. This can be most simply seen from two primitive logical facts:

(1) *consistency* is required of a thinker on any subject matter: to show that a naturalist or historian or eye-witness has contradicted himself is to show that his account of what he has undertaken to describe or explain is necessarily false (where this means that it contains some element or elements which are *false* in a non-logical sense). Philosophers and others sometimes fall into a confusion here between two different uses of the expression 'necessarily false'. By saying that an account is necessarily false I may mean that it has the logical property of internal contradiction; that it contains elements which are in logical conflict with other elements, so that the joint assertion of its various elements is logically illegitimate. But I may say that if p is true then q is necessarily false where what I mean is that the falsehood of q necessarily follows from the truth of p, even though p and q are both contingent propositions. The distinction has sometimes been marked by speaking of *necessitas consequentiae* as opposed to *necessitas consequentis*.

(2) Every enquiry into the truth or falsehood of a proposition, or into the acceptability or unacceptability of an utterance of any kind, involves logic in this further respect: that the purpose of the enquiry is to determine which of two or more incompatible propositions (or whatever is expressed by the relevant non-propositional utterances) is to be accepted and which rejected. In every sphere in which rational enquiry is possible at all, the method to be followed in order to secure the determination of the question will be one or other form of presentation of argument or evidence. Now the effect of argument and evidence, when it *is* effective – one might say instead, when it

is *argument* or *evidence* – is to force the person to whom it is addressed to choose between incompatibles, not only strategically and ultimately, but also tactically and intermediately. It is not just that the ultimate outcome of the enquiry, if it is successful, is to establish *p* as opposed to not-*p*, but that an analogous choice has to be made at each step on the way, as each argument or piece of evidence is adduced. At each such stage, even if the argument or evidence is not such as to require on pain of contradiction that we choose between rejecting the argument or evidence and accepting the conclusion to which it points, it will require us, if it is an argument or evidence for its conclusion, to choose between strengthening our confidence in the conclusion and rejecting its claim to be argument or evidence. Even when a reason is not a logically conclusive reason, and hence not one that can be denied only by one who *ipso facto* denies the relevant conclusion, it is always such that one must either reject it or accept that there is ground for greater confidence in the truth of the conclusion than there would be in the absence of the reason. This necessity is also a triviality, but its necessity is so important for our present purpose that its triviality does not matter. What we are always trying to do when we reason with another is to face him with choices between making concessions to our favoured conclusion and denying something that, as he recognises, there is strong reason not to deny. We present him with evidence or argument that we expect *him* to regard as cogent against what he himself has said, and so to reveal an inconsistency between what he has said and something else that he believes or knows.

It may need emphasising that the structure of an investigation is not altered by the fact that it is conducted by a single individual, not in debate or contest with another or others. If I am halting between two opinions, and reflecting on the grounds on which I may rationally be brought to fix my belief on one side or the other, I am faced at every step with a choice of the same kind as in a dialectical exchange I shall hope to present to my opponent.

The substitution of concrete examples for this abstract framework firmly underlines the main point that the coherence theorists have bequeathed to us. That London Bridge is or is not burning down is a contingent truth or falsehood. It is not a truth or falsehood of logic that Old Mother Hubbard's cupboard is or is not bare. But when I am debating with you or with myself the question which of each of these pairs of propositions is true, I may find my mind forced by the sight and sound of crackling flames or of empty shelves and a whining dog.

The structure of disagreement that is illustrated here is applicable in all fields of investigation. 'Twitting with inconsistency' is a form of challenge that is not specific to ethical or any other species of argumentation. It is nevertheless worth while, in a book of moral philosophy, to explore more fully the application of this structure to moral debate. Such an exploration will do little or nothing to characterise what is distinctive about morality, but it will still help to characterise morality, whose character, like that of everything else, consists largely of characteristics that are not peculiar to it. It will also help us to resist what we have already seen to be persuasive attempts to represent morality as differing more than it does from some or all non-moral enquiries.

This combination of purposes can be well served by returning to the sentence from Hume's *Enquiry* that has so often been the clarion call of the ethical subjectivist: 'After every circumstance, every relation is known, the reason has no further room to operate, nor any object on which it could employ itself.' The sentence has commonly been used to express what is distinctive about ethics, and it is one form of words in which it is possible to mark what we have seen to be the logical peculiarity of evaluative judgements. Yet it does so misleadingly, and we have needed the help of numerous other theoretical formulations, as well as some detailed descriptions of examples, in order to give sufficient and yet not undue emphasis to the contrasts that are to be drawn between evaluation, factual investigation, and logical reflection. Now that that part of the work of Hume's sentence is done, we may notice another way in which it can be used in our investigation, but only if we see it to have implications quite different from those ordinarily attributed to it by subjectivist philosophers, even if not by Hume himself. For such philosophers have misrepresented a situation that in some respects they have so accurately described. They have given the false impression that at the final stage, when all questions of fact and of logic have been agreed between us, we are just beginning to deal with the serious moral question that divides us. They have supposed that this position is one that we commonly reach; that we are familiar with disputes in which the parties are divided by serious moral issues, but in which at the same time they are fully agreed on the factual and logical issues that are relevant to their moral disagreement. My objections to this supposition were outlined when I dealt in Chapter 2 with the standard arguments for subjectivism, and especially with the argument from disagreement and the argument from the assumption that there is a peculiarly moral ingredient, and that nothing that does not consist entirely of this ingredient is moral at all. In the light of what we have noticed in succeeding chapters the same objection can now be elaborated and presented with greater clarity and force.

In many of the cases commonly taken to illustrate stark moral disagreement, accompanied by full agreement on facts and logic, there is agreement on important and relevant questions of value. Since the disagreements that best suit the sceptic's purpose are disagreements about choices between the horns of stark moral dilemmas, it is natural that this should be so. For whatever one may think of the definition of tragedy as 'the conflict of right with right', a moral dilemma is constituted by an inescapable need to choose between two rights or two wrongs, two goods or two evils, and the supposed conflict between warring moralities will not be intelligible as such except to one who recognises the force of each of the conflicting claims. Agamemnon can agonise about his choice between the sacrifice of Iphigeneia and the sacrifice of the expedition against Troy, and we can make sense, as spectators, of his tragedy, only because he and we can see and feel the killing of a child and the betrayal of a sacred trust as crimes, as sins, and as disasters. And it makes no difference to the present point whether the dilemma afflicts a single agent such as Agamemnon, or is the subject, as Agamemnon's choice can easily be, of a dispute between two persons or two parties. D. Z. Phillips and II. O. Mounce (*Moral Practices*, pp. 58–9) make use of an example from a modern controversy. A 'scientific rationalist' may urge the use of contraceptives on a Catholic mother, overburdened with children, whose loyalty to her faith, her priest, her Pope, prompts her to resist the tempting persuasion. But there would be no dilemma and no conflict, no grief and no temptation, if it were not seen on both sides that poverty and overcrowding are evils and misfortunes, that disloyalty may be a pain as well as a sin, that a woman may be unhappy because she has too many children or unhappy because she is barred from the sacraments, that children may suffer from a mother's unhappiness regardless of its cause, and so on as far as our experience and imagination will take us.

When Sartre presents the case of the young man who has to choose between supporting his mother and supporting the struggle for freedom against tyranny he represents himself as supporting the conclusion that moral judgements express unreasoned choices, that there are no marks for our guidance, that 'every man is condemned at every instant to invent man'. Yet Sartre is able to paint the dilemma in considerable detail, and each detail is itself a sample of the moral knowledge that Sartre is trying to deny to us. In showing or saying that one consideration balances another he reveals his own recognition of the nature and force of the various considerations, and appeals to our own recognition of their nature and force.

Sartre's treatment of the example is a skilful display of philosophical sleight of hand, and it no doubt deceives its author as deeply as it has deceived any reader. The conclusion is supposed to be that if a conflict is a *moral* conflict then it will necessarily be like the stark dilemma that has been described. Wherever the man turns for advice he cannot be given anything but an ungrounded declaration that one side or the other is to be preferred. He can only choose, that is to say, invent. Because the considerations *exactly* balance, it is foolish to look for anything on either side that can outweigh what is found on the other. And all moral choices are equally untrammelled by ground or precedent. We are always and everywhere condemned to invent man; we have inherited nothing in our values, either from the history of the human race or from our own individual histories. And yet the whole story of the dilemma is unintelligible except as constituting an evenly balanced conflict between *recognised* values. A being who did not see that a man should try to support his mother rather than see her starve or grieve to death, or who did not see that tyranny is to be resisted rather than tolerated, or who failed to recognise the moral force of any of the other claims whose conflict Sartre exploits, would not understand the dilemma as a dilemma. The presentation of the dilemma presupposes the moral values that it is designed to overthrow. Sartre recognises, and knows that we can be expected to recognise, the force of those agreed values, founded upon the fabric and constitution of the human species, to which he must implicitly appeal in order to place before us a dilemma whose explicit purpose is to persuade us that we know nothing about morality at all.

The examples offered by Sartre and by Phillips and

Mounce are disqualified in another way for the role in which they are cast, and in this respect too they are typical of their kind. The intention was to produce cases in which there are no agreed values, but in which everything *but* values *is* agreed. The cases actually produced fail the second test as clearly as they fail the first. Not only do they fail to be cases in which there is no agreement on values; they also fail to be cases in which there is agreement on facts and logic; and the unresolved issues of fact and logic have an agreed bearing on the unresolved moral disagreement. Two people do not agree on everything but values if one of them believes that St Peter was given the power to bind and loose and the other thinks that all religion is superstition or that the only religious authority is Holy Writ or the individual consciences of a priesthood of all believers. The collaborationist who advises Sartre's young man to stay at home does not agree with the resistance worker who advises the young man to go to war about how effective the resistance will be or how tyrannically the Germans will behave as the war goes on or how soon there will be a second front. And it is clear from Sartre's own account that uncertainties about matters of fact are some of the bones of the structure of the student's dilemma. Will he ever reach the Free French Headquarters, and if he does, what will he achieve? Will he spend the rest of the war in internment, or filling forms in an office far from the front?

Hume himself gives examples that are subject to the same comments. The morally relevant difference between my apples and those of my neighbour is not perceptible at a glance like a difference of colour or shape, but it is none-theless a difference concerning a matter of fact: he has bought the house and garden with the tree standing in it, or he has bought the tree and planted it in his own garden. The oak tree and the sapling show some of the relations that obtain between Nero and Agrippina, but not all and not the most relevant to our moral judgement upon the emperor's crime of matricide. If the tree and the sapling were endowed as the mother and son are with minds and hearts and consciousness and memory and passions and sentiments and personal histories and social relations they would become morally comparable with them, but would for the same reasons be rendered liable to commendation and condemnation for their acts and omissions.

The inadequacy of an attempt to account for morality entirely in terms of any narrowly conceived passions or sentiments of approbation and disapprobation is revealed if we compare a typical moral issue with a difference that really does hinge on a mere attitude of liking or disliking, attraction or repulsion. Most Englishmen do not eat snails or frogs' legs, and many Englishmen, when on visits to France or to French restaurants, are unwilling even to taste either of these delicacies. Questions of gastronomic taste may be involved here, but we can easily isolate a different factor: a revulsion, no doubt born of unfamiliarity and of proverbial condemnation of an alien cuisine, which has nothing to do with a dislike of the flavours of the despised dishes. There are stories, which are convincing even if they are not true, of English people who enjoyed eating what was set before them until they were told that it was *escargots* or frogs' legs, and were then sick. The hero of such a story will not willingly accept the same dish again, even if he has no moral or gastronomic objection to the offending food.

The revulsion in these cases is at least a close approximation to the isolated and unreasoned response of the heart with which some philosophers have tried to identify moral disapprobation. The identification loses all its plausibility as soon as we compare the revulsion against frogs or snails with objections that do have in them some tincture of the moral. If we change the example to songbirds in Italy, and therefore add an 'ecological' or conservationist consideration to the account, the matter at once becomes open to discussion and argument. By the time we reach full-scale vegetarianism we have also reached full-scale moral disagreement, with all the potentialities it brings with it of reflection and investigation, argument and evidence, twitting with inconsistency and ignorance. The point is sharpened if we notice that even a complete vegetarianism *may* be based on a mere revulsion like that of the insular Englishman against frogs: but in that case, by the very fact of no longer allowing for argument, it disqualifies itself from being a moral position and becomes instead a mere reaction, to be sharply contrasted rather than closely compared with any typical moral attitude or opinion.

One of the sources of the illusion that we may and commonly do agree on questions of fact and logic while still disagreeing about questions of value is a mistake about the scope of the notion of a question of fact, and another is a mistake about the scope of the notion of a question of logic. Hume made both mistakes, and it is therefore natural that his work should contain remarks and phrases that are encouraging and useful to the sceptic. The mistake consists in each case of restricting the scope of the concept by treating one particular type of example as paradigmatic, and excluding all others for their failure to conform to a specification derived from the supposed paradigms. Hume has been followed in the commission of these mistakes, as in many things, by twentieth-century positivist philosophers, and the mistakes have been repeatedly diagnosed by critics of positivism. But the negative task of exposing the positivists' errors has not usually been accompanied by a sufficiently full and clear positive characterisation of the concepts that have suffered at their hands.

If we try to answer in general terms the question 'What is a question of fact?' we are likely to think first of cases in which observation or experiment is called for, and to use such cases as the basis for framing a definition or criterion, or directly as paradigms, for the application of the term 'question of fact' in general. Yet it is easy to show that there may be a dispute about a question of fact between two parties who agree on the results of all the relevant observations and experiments. I may accept the grocer's statement that I owe him £1.73 for bacon and £2.30 for butter and £7.10 for tinned goods while denying his statement that I owe him £11.43 altogether. I accuse him of making an arithmetical mistake, rather than of mis-stating a particular matter of fact about the price or quantity of one of the items, but in denying his claim that I owe him £11.43 I am nevertheless disagreeing with him about a matter of fact. In spite of its extreme simplicity, this example is decisive against the suggestion, often explicitly made and more often implicitly relied on, that we cannot be disagreeing about a matter of fact if we agree on 'the facts' in the narrower sense of the raw data bearing on the question we are considering. When we acknowledge the range and variety of cases for which this simple case opens the way, we can see how easily the imposition of a restrictive definition could blind a philosopher to the complexities of the questions of fact that were still at issue between two parties who had reached a reflective rather than an observational or experimental phase of their controversy.

The range of possibilities is dramatically widened as soon as we pass from cases of pure calculation to those involving reflection on the application of more informal concepts, whether or not they are moral concepts: not only *theft* or *negligence* or *jealousy* or *disloyalty*, but *contentment* or *nostalgia* or *standard of living* or *baroque*. Whether an instance does or does not fall under one of these concepts may be a question of fact about the instance, even if the determination of that question at this stage calls for informal reflection rather than for empirical observation or experiment.

The comparison of these examples with that of the grocer's bill also serves to illustrate the restriction that has often been imposed on the notion of a question of logic, what Hume calls a question concerning 'relations of ideas'.

The informal reflection that we may have to undertake in order to determine whether an action is treacherous or a novel picaresque or a man malicious is *a priori* even though it is not a process of calculation. We are concerned with questions of logic or the relations of ideas whenever we ask whether such and such a description of an instance (perhaps a detailed and extended account of the circumstances and origins and effects of an action) is good or sufficient grounds for the application to that instance of such and such another description (perhaps a compendious epithet like *ambitious* or a summary verdict like *guilty*).

The scope of this last observation is wide enough to cover any case in which what is at issue is the question whether something does or does not fall under a particular concept. Every such question is or includes an *a priori* question about the relation between a characterisation of the thing and a characterisation of the concept. The characterisation of the concept may be in the form of a definition, but it will not in that case be in its fundamental form. For a definition is a formulation of the structure of the use of a term, and the formulation is correct or incorrect according to whether it accurately or inaccurately presents the structure. A common failing among definitions is to oversimplify for the sake of memorability and orderliness. But whether a definition is accurate or inaccurate, tidy or untidy, the test of its validity is an examination of the instances to which the defined term is applicable. An instance can show that a definition is mistaken, but a definition cannot show that an instance does not fall under the term unless there is a way of showing that it does not fall under the term that does not depend on the definition.

Both the applicability or inapplicability of a term to an instance and the accuracy or inaccuracy of a definition of a term can be tested if at all by comparisons and contrasts between instances. As Peirce puts it in an essay on 'The Century's Great Men in Science' (*Values in a Universe of Chance*, p. 265):

Amid these differences of opinion any definition of greatness would be like a disputed rule of grammar. Just as a rule of grammar does not render an expression bad English, but only generalizes the fact that good writers do not use it, so, in order to establish a definition of greatness it would be necessary to begin by ascertaining what men were and what men were not great and that having been done the rule might as well be dispensed with.

We have arrived by a rather different route at an alternative partial description of what Broad was partially describing when he spoke of 'twitting with inconsistency'. The same procedure of argument has been still partially but slightly more fully described by F. R. Leavis when he has said that in criticism what happens in the end is that one man says 'This is so, isn't it?' and the other replies 'Yes, but ...'. Leavis is thinking of discussion of works of literature, and of lines and words in them, conducted with a high degree of particularity. His description applies equally well to any discussion that proceeds, as all discussion does in the last resort, by comparison and contrast of particular instances with particular instances. In the last resort, wherever there is conflict about what is so, about what is true or false, good or bad, right or wrong, there is scope for the same appeal, 'This is so, isn't it?', and the same rejoinder, 'Yes, but ...'. But this summary is faithful to the ultimate character of conflict only because it also brings to light that the conflict is between parties who also *agree*. Not only does the 'Yes' of the respondent's 'Yes, but ...' signify agreement, but the 'but' itself draws attention to something that can also be recognised by the author of the original 'This is so, isn't it?'. The 'but' itself is a new 'This is so, isn't it?' and may call for another answering 'Yes, but ...'. Here we have the shape that qualifies moral discussion and critical discussion and philosophical discussion and in the last resort all discussion to be called by the ancient name of *dialectic*. We can represent the complexity that such fundamental enquiry deals with, without becoming bewildered by the maze of detail, only if we give this dialectical structure to our strivings after understanding of the detail. And this remains true whatever the scale of the operation, from the minute examination of one of Virgil's half-lines to the vast scale on which the philosopher may sometimes operate, and on which we should try to operate, I have been suggesting, when we seek a comprehensive grasp of the nature of moral enquiry.

When we set up an intuitionist or rationalist theory against an emotivist one, when we set up Kant against Hume, we are still dealing with the same structure, still trying, however much greater the scale, to achieve a three-dimensional grasp of a three-dimensional structure by using the tried method of the stereoscope. You will see a three-dimensional representation of the Parthenon only if you are presented with two different pictures from two different angles. The same principle of method is available to us in philosophy. If you give your signature exclusively to one theory you condemn yourself to incompleteness of vision. If you work dialectically then by grasping the import and upshot of a theory you are not debarring yourself from grasping the upshot and import of another theory that is a rival to it. In the pursuit of an understanding that is in the end non-theoretical, not expressed in slogan or manifesto, we may justifiably and rewardingly use the conflicting theories as instruments.

I have accordingly made use of some of the terms and propositions associated with some of the traditional and current theories of ethics. In particular, I have repeatedly endorsed an 'objectivist' view of the nature of moral argument and moral conflict. But all such theorising and all such theoretical terms are theoretically dispensable, and even when we use them our aim should be – as it often unconsciously is – to achieve or restore or articulate a non-theoretical understanding of the intricacies that the theoretical statements simultaneously summarise and distort. To hold that no theory gives us the whole truth is not to say that no theory gives us any of the truth, and still less to say that there is no truth to give and to receive. We need not deny, as we throw away the shells, that the oysters were succulent and nutritious, even if we allow or insist that there are other and plainer sources of nourishment.

CHAPTER 7

ARGUMENT

'Logic is the ethics of the intellect.' This remark by C. S. Peirce in a letter to Lady Welby (*Values in a Universe of Chance*, p. 415) points in the same direction as his better known characterisation of logic as 'a normative science' (*Collected Papers*, vol. IV, § 240). The less familiar formulation has richer implications, and makes a better starting point for the last stage of an enquiry into the similarities and differences between moral and non-moral reasoning. For one can compendiously say much of what remains to be said by transposing the terms of Peirce's compendious comment: 'Ethics is the logic of the will and the emotions.'

Logical validity is a *value*. An argument that has it is, other things being equal, a *good* argument, one that is sound and reliable and useful. In its role as the ethics of the understanding, logic guides us in doing those things that we ought to do, and leaving undone the things that we ought not to do. Logic deals, as ethics does, in the coinage of good and bad and right and wrong. The comparison is convertible into the observation that ethics is concerned with validity and truth; that the appraisals and assessments that it calls for, or of which it consists, are also subject to appraisal and assessment by rigorously rational procedures.

When the dual comparison is made in terms as general and as colourful as those used and prompted by Peirce's aphorism it will sound either obscure or extravagant to

those who have not looked for themselves in the direction in
which he and we are pointing. A similar gesture that is liable
to cause similar bewilderment to those whom it does not
immediately enlighten is Wisdom's remark to a student
(*Philosophy and Psycho-Analysis*, p. 217):

> About a year ago I was talking to a man who had been
> reading that ethical statements really express our feelings.
> Some philosophers have spoken as if we cannot show an
> ethical statement to be correct or find it incorrect. This sort
> of thing had led to or increased in this man a feeling of
> despair, a feeling that nothing really matters, a feeling that
> the world is water, without form and void. And this was not
> a man with a 'half-baked' acquaintance with the meta-ethics
> that affected him. I said to him, 'Suppose the goodness of a
> person were as objective as the goodness of an argument.'

Ayer, on p. 35 of *The Origins of Pragmatism*, comments on
the 'somewhat peculiar usage' according to which Peirce
makes both logic and ethics subordinate to aesthetics, i.e. to
'the normative science that concerns itself with ultimate
ends'. Yet this subordination would show almost by itself
that Peirce had seen what Ayer and many others have failed
to see: that value, far from being contrasted with fact and
logic as swamp with firm ground, or little sister with big
twin brothers, is more fundamental than either, so that Plato
might well have declared the Form of the Good to be *epekeina
tēs praxeōs* as well as *epekeina tēs ousias*: a value that is neither
practical nor theoretical is prior to being and truth, action
and choice. Neither logic nor history nor physics nor
philosophy nor any other sphere in which this is *preferred* to
that, where one view may and must be compared in *soundness*
with another, where reasons may be adjudged good or bad,
strong or weak, can be a point of vantage from which a
philosopher may look down on the concept of value, unless
we take the talk of looking down to mark the necessary but
rare recognition that here if anywhere is the bedrock in
search of which so many philosophers have scanned the sky.

Fortunately we can set out the same points without the high colour and broad generality that may befog the vision of their cogency, and in a way that nevertheless preserves a recognition of their scope. It has been fashionable among subjectivist moral philosophers to make use of the distinction between *is* and *ought*. It is argued that the premises of a moral argument, once it has been reduced to a form in which it is not question-begging, must be propositions about what *is* the case: for example, about the details of actions or circumstances or causal consequences or motives or characters. A moral conclusion, on the other hand, is a proposition about what *ought* to be the case, and no such conclusion can be the logical consequence of a set of premises none of which is itself evaluative rather than factual or descriptive. If the premises of a moral argument do include a moral proposition, then the subjectivist will argue that the question has been begged against him, since his sceptical question relates to evaluation in general and as such, and hence to every evaluative proposition that could be used as a premise as much as to the conclusion in whose support it might be invoked.

The comparison made by Peirce and Wisdom suggests a reply to this familiar type of argument. Far from its being the case that we cannot argue from *is* premises to an *ought* conclusion, this is a feat that we repeatedly perform in a context in which it would not occur to the sceptic or subjectivist himself to doubt its legitimacy, and indeed in a form that he must countenance if his own argument against objectivism is to deserve even *prima facie* consideration. For his argument, like every argument, purports to be *valid*, sound, cogent, compelling. It is the whole point of an argument that it should exercise constraint on one who accepts its premises. If for example he agrees that p and q, and if p and q are sufficient reasons for r, then he ought to accept the truth of r. And the principle of such an argument is precisely a statement to the effect that premises of a certain sort are sufficient for the truth of a conclusion of a certain sort. (There are of course arguments of many other kinds, but they need not be considered here, both because a simple deductive argument is all that we need for making the present point, and because the point could in any case be made, though inevitably in a more complex form, by means of examples of more complex forms of argument.)

Consider then the conclusion that I *ought* to recognise or acknowledge the truth of *r*. This is a (logically) evaluative conclusion; it could be expressed in a number of other but all equally clearly evaluative forms: the argument for the conclusion *r* is good, sound, cogent, convincing, conclusive, strong, irrefutable. What is the basis of the claim that I *ought* to accept *r*? It may be said that I ought to accept it because of the validity of the argument for it, but this at once raises a question exactly like the sceptic's question about the validity of moral arguments. To say that the argument is valid, or to cite in its support a rule to the effect that arguments of such and such a form are valid, is to support the evaluative conclusion that I ought to accept the argument by an evaluative premise, and therefore to beg the question against a sceptic about deductive argument in any sense in which the moral sceptic is entitled to claim that the question is begged against him by the moralist or philosopher who supports moral conclusions by offering moral premises. In logic, as in ethics, when we seek the ultimate or fundamental grounds of an evaluative conclusion, we must seek them among premises that are not themselves evaluative. A *philosophical* question about the nature of validity or cogency or logical compulsion is a question about a logical rule as well as about any particular argument that it may be said to validate; it is a question about any logically evaluative expression that may appear in the premises of an argument as well as about any conclusion that is expressed in a logically evaluative . form.

In defending the validity of logical rules in general against a sceptic about logical argument, we should need to do what we recognise in our practice to be appropriate when we are defending the validity of a particular logical rule or of a particular argument falling under it. We move from the mere endorsement of the validity of the argument or its principle to the description and presentation of the *form* of the argument. And there is no more a non-question-begging way of deductively deriving a conclusion about the validity of an argument from its form than there is a non-question-begging way of deductively deriving a conclusion about the morality of an action from a purely factual or 'descriptive' account of the action. It follows that if the ultimate justification of logical rules or the validity of logical arguments is required to be deductive it will be just as circular or regressive as the ultimate justification of any other mode of enquiry of which the same condition is exacted.

The remedy is not to despair of offering a justification but to reject the troublesome condition. It is self-defeating to attempt to impose a requirement which must necessarily fail to be satisfied by every conceivable attempt to provide a justification: and it is clear that every attempted justification must necessarily *either* be deductive and therefore based on premises of the same kind as the conclusion which it undertakes to justify, *or* be based on premises which are different in kind from the conclusion that it undertakes to justify and therefore be non-deductive.

The self-defeatingness of the sceptic's requirement is even more radical than we have so far recognised. He must reject everything that we could conceivably offer in justification of any conclusion; for every possible justification will either meet his deductive requirement and hence raise again all the questions that it was intended to settle, or it will fail to meet this requirement and therefore fail to amount to what he

calls a justification. By imposing these absurd conditions the
sceptic inadvertently guides us towards an account of what *is*
acceptable – though not of course to him – as an
understanding of the ultimate grounds of knowledge.

The parallels between theoretical and practical reason are
so numerous and extensive that we can turn the tables on
almost any argument that a sceptic about practical
knowledge may adduce. They are accordingly so numerous
and extensive that we need an explanation of why
philosophers have so persistently succumbed to the illusion
of a wide gulf between theory and practice. The principle of
the explanation is provided by the description we have
already given of the peculiarity of evaluative reasoning,
which is exaggerated and misrepresented because it *is* a
peculiarity. Analogously, the asymmetry of the verification
of psychological propositions, or the corrigibility in
principle of propositions about material objects, or the
necessary indirectness of the validation of propositions
about the past or the future, is repeatedly made into a
ground for demeaning or overlooking the extensive
parallels between each of these classes of propositions and
those with which philosophers have been concerned to
contrast them. This danger is endemic in epistemology, but
in recent decades there have been particular and local
reasons why it has been a specially troublesome obstacle to
our getting a clear view of the fundamental kinship between
theoretical and practical reasoning. Philosophers in this
continent in this century have been engaged in a battle
against *psychologism* in logic. Their determination has been to
distinguish the psychology of judgement and belief from the
logic of argument and inference, and from the tactics of
debate that have traditionally been investigated by rhetoric
and dialectic and similar non-formal studies of the skills of
argument and advocacy.

This battle against psychologism has been no more than
half won. It will not be concluded until the logic of practical

reasoning – and of history, sociology, criticism, theology – is as free of it as the logic of deduction and induction. The emotions or attitudes of approval, resentment, guilt, hope, fear, hate and love, jealousy and envy, humility and pride, are no more (but also no less) constitutive of moral and critical rationality than the acts, emotions and attitudes that belong to theoretical enquiry are its constituents or foundations: such acts and emotions and attitudes as asserting and denying, believing and disbelieving, confidence and doubt, hope and fear, conviction, expectation and astonishment. No more – but also no less: the campaign to induce us not to exaggerate the relevance to theoretical enquiry of states of mind and human actions has led some of us not only to exaggerate the dependence of practical enquiry on psychological states and actions but also to minimise the relevance of such states and actions to theoretical enquiry itself. It will therefore be useful to supplement the discussion of the place of reason in ethics by some consideration of the place of action and attitude in logic, and in particular by noticing the applicability to theory of two specific concepts. The first is recognised to have a place in the realm of theory but thought to belong primarily to practice. The second has never to my knowledge been allowed to have any place in theoretical enquiry at all.

The analogy between moral evaluation and logical evaluation is shown to be complete when we notice the involvement in logic as in ethics of the notion of *commitment*. If I accept the premises of a valid argument I commit myself to accepting the conclusion. I may accept premises from which a particular consequence follows and yet fail to accept that consequence. In that case I shall be guilty of the logical fault of inconsistency, and it is noteworthy that one way of diagnosing this fault is to say that in such a case I am *committed* to accepting something that I nevertheless do not accept. In the give and take or cut and thrust of a dialectical debate I may similarly accept, but unwillingly, that I am

committed to such and such a position that I had not seen
for myself to be a consequence of a thesis to which I had
consciously committed myself.

The relevance of the concept of commitment to contexts
of logical argument as well as to those of moral judgement
and action extends further the parallel between theory and
practice which is already shown to be extensive by the
analogies we have perceived between approval and belief,
action and assertion, emotions and propositional attitudes.
The unfitness of the familiar contrasts between theoretical
and practical reasoning to be the grounds of moral
scepticism is even more emphatically displayed when we
notice the room that these last similarities provide for the
operation on the theoretical side of the boundary of
something that is familiar in moral and other practical
contexts under the name of *akrasia*. This is the second of the
two concepts it will be useful to consider.

Moral *akrasia* is a combination of moral recognition with
failure to act in accordance with the relevant practical
conclusion. Socrates identified virtue with knowledge, and
construed knowledge as necessarily intellectual or
theoretical, and accordingly concluded that *akrasia* was
impossible. Aristotle's conception of practical reasoning as
akin to but distinct from theoretical reasoning allowed him
to hold that Socrates was partly right while still rejecting the
main force of the Socratic paradox. The *phronimos* is *praktikos*:
full *practical* understanding necessarily cannot be attributed
to one who does not *act* appropriately, however clear and
explicit his theoretical conviction may be. The practical
understanding of the morally virtuous man involves sincere
performance of what is right in a sense analogous to that in
which *sophia* or *epistēmē* involves sincere assent to what is true,
and full understanding of the truth that is expressed. On the
practical side of the comparison there is the further
requirement that the agent (or 'patient') should feel
appropriately: the courageous man enjoys the exercise of

courage, while the man who is not yet courageous, though he may act courageously, will do so with a struggle and at the cost of some distress.

In his discussion of *akrasia* Aristotle makes use of his usual distinction between potentiality and actuality. My knowledge of one of the premises in a practical argument may be latent rather than active, so that I can be said to know it but not to know it in the full sense. It may accordingly be right to say of me that I do what I know to be wrong, and yet to save an important element in the Socratic paradox by adding that my knowledge falls short of being full and active knowledge. Aristotle makes a comparison with the man who is mad or drunk and still quotes verses of Empedocles.

It has not been noticed that there is scope on the theoretical side for a phenomenon closely comparable with practical *akrasia*, which it may be convenient to describe as theoretical *akrasia*. A woman may 'hope against hope' that her child will recover from leukaemia or poliomyelitis when there is no ground for optimism, and when she knows that there is no such ground. A wife may be capable of seeing the force of the evidence against her refusal to admit that her husband, reported to be 'missing believed killed', will never return. The ambitious man may not be willing to face the fact that he will not succeed in his ambition to be Prime Minister or an Olympic athlete or a leading concert pianist. In all these cases the subject or victim of the *akrasia* may be as capable as any critic or companion of tracing out the structure and assessing the weight of the evidence that convicts him of being unreasonable: the analogy with moral or practical *akrasia* is close precisely because in theoretical as in practical reflection there is something to *do* as well as something to consider or contemplate: an act of admitting or acknowledging what has happened or is happening or will happen, of bearing an uncomfortable reality and renouncing a soothing illusion. We notice or allege a case of theoretical *akrasia* whenever we speak of *refusing* to see, of not *wanting* to know, and in at least some of the cases where we accuse someone of self-deception, or of living in a fool's paradise. Whatever may be the rights and wrongs of the disputes between Descartes and his critics, and between William James and W. K. Clifford, it is clear that at a decisive stage in a process of theoretical or factual reflection there is scope for exercise or atrophy of the will, and for the emotions to amount to high obstacles against the drawing of a true conclusion.

Peirce is endorsing the use made here of his remarks about the ethics of the intellect when he speaks in another passage of the exercise of 'logical self-control' (*Collected Papers*, vol. V, §440). That is the intellectual-and-moral virtue whose absence is what I have called theoretical *akrasia*.

The general lesson of these examples for the moral philosopher is confirmed rather than weakened if we notice the difficulty of drawing a clear line between instances of theoretical and of practical *akrasia*. My hesitation to step on to the ice may be a manifestation of doubt about its firmness, or of nervousness even in the face of conditions I know to be safe; but there is an intermediate or mixed case in which my failure to draw from adequate evidence the correct conclusion that the ice is safe is itself a symptom of lack of confidence rather than a lack of competence at judging the conditions. William James, in support of his thesis that 'our passional and volitional nature' not only actually does, but legitimately may influence our opinions on questions of what is true and what is false, describes a case in which each individual passenger on a train offers no resistance to invading robbers because he believes that the other passengers would fail to support him, whereas if he believed that it was possible to resist, they would support him and it would then be possible to overcome the invaders (*The Will to Believe and Other Essays*, p. 24). This example again presents a mixture of theoretical and practical *akrasia*, and so helps to underline the parallels between the two species.

The situation discussed by James lends itself to description in betting terms, and certainly literal cases of betting, with their characteristic mingling of judgement or misjudgement of facts and odds with attitudes and emotions of expectation, hope and fear, serve well to illustrate the parallels we have been considering. The gambler may make a miscalculation of the odds, or misread a horse's form, or be misled by a usually reliable source, but not all the mistakes that he makes will be of these relatively unproblematic factual and logical kinds. He may know that the odds are against him and yet throw good money after bad because of ordinary moral *akrasia*, and he may also be subject to theoretical *akrasia*: for example, he may so much want to win this hand against this opponent that he refuses to allow his latent understanding of the cards and of the opponent to become savingly active, and may thus embrace a disaster that is not revealed to him by what he now believes.

There is further scope for both theoretical and practical *akrasia*, and hence also for mixed and borderline cases of this kind, in conversation, discussion, and reflection or deliberation even when it is conducted by an individual communing with himself. A man may disguise his recognition that he has lost the point or the argument, or he may simply fail to see that his position has been damaged; but there is also the case in which his desire for victory or for security in a cherished conviction blinds him to the truth that his mind would grasp if it were not for the intervention of his will. I may deceive myself into avoiding an unwelcome theoretical or practical conclusion even when my discussion is with myself alone. From the time of Socrates and the oracle at Delphi we have known of the importance and the difficulty of self-knowledge: in the pursuit of it we need all the intellectual and moral virtues that we need in any other strenuous enquiry, and hence it allows the scope that all the others allow for *akrasia* of mind and heart.

This consideration of *akrasia* reinforces some of the points made in Chapter 4 in connection with Newell's contrast between departmental and interdepartmental problems of epistemology. Since one's own peace of mind and self-respect are so largely involved in questions about one's moral character and actions, it is natural that failure to face facts should be specially common in contexts of moral perplexity or disagreement. But such failure is also common in cases that have nothing to do with morality, and where it is evident that the facts that are not being faced are straightforward non-moral facts. It follows that the possibility of such failure is no objection to the objectivity of the questions at issue, and therefore that the phenomenon of moral *akrasia* is not part of what distinguishes the logic of moral enquiry from that of other enquiries. We can nevertheless, as in discussing the relation of disagreement to objectivity, preserve our recognition that there are logically distinctive features of morality, in spite of recognising also that subjective theorists have repeatedly identified as one of them something that is in fact found equally clearly, even if not equally frequently, in non-moral reflection.

The involvement of desires and emotions in ethics is no more of an obstacle to the interpersonal objectivity of moral enquiry than the involvement of desires and emotions in other enquiries defeats their claims to be branches of objective knowledge. This conclusion, which we have presented more than once with backing from more than one direction, may now be further clarified and supported in the light of the increasingly extensive parallelism we have observed between the theoretical and the practical employments of the human understanding. The main lessons to be drawn from the parallelism can usefully be presented in a parallel discussion of the moral sceptic's traditional challenge 'Why should I be moral?', or 'Why should I do what is right?' and formulations of a wider sceptical challenge which echo the sound of their morally sceptical analogues: 'Why should I believe what is true?', or 'Why should I be reasonable?', or 'Why should I argue validly?'

Each of these questions may be understood in at least three different ways, and may therefore attract at least three different kinds of response. One possible reaction to the question 'Why should I believe what is true?' is to declare that the question is absurd and self-stultifying. To be true precisely is to be worthy to be believed, to be a proper object of belief, and hence to ask a question which implies that something can be identified as true while there still remains a doubt or hesitation about whether it is to be believed is to be involved in absurdity. The question 'Why should I argue validly?', construed in an analogous manner, invites the analogous reply that it is absurd to characterise a particular way of arguing as logical – where this is not merely a specification of the type of subject matter of the argument but an assessment of its cogency – and still to regard it as an unsettled question whether that way of arguing is to be adopted or endorsed.

The questions 'Why should I do what is right?' and 'Why should I be moral?' have been dealt with on similar lines by many defenders of an objective conception of morality. If I am satisfied that an action is correctly described as *the right thing to do*, then it seems absurd that I should still be asking why I should do that action, since in order to be satisfied that it is right I need already to be satisfied that it is *the thing to do*.

But it is clear in the cases of the epistemological and logical challenges, and perhaps even clearer in the case of the moral challenge, that the effect of this first type of response is mainly to secure some negative clarification of the nature of the challenge, and only indirectly and marginally to achieve anything towards an answer to it. It is easy for the moral challenger to rephrase his challenge as '*Is* anything right?' or 'Can anything be known or shown to be right?' There are corresponding forms of words that the epistemological and logical challengers could use: '*Is* anything true, or valid?', 'How can I know or show that there is truth, or logical validity, in any particular proposition or argument?' When the challenges are presented in these forms they can no longer be represented as expressions of mere confusion. They now do clearly raise philosophical questions that are interesting and difficult. Yet it is still not clear *what* questions they raise, and we can only become clear about this if we draw further distinctions between possible uses of the original forms of words which are paralleled by alternative uses of the revised formulations.

The challenges in the new forms are explicitly epistemological or justificational, or – we might say if the word had not acquired doctrinal associations and also come to imply a restriction to a limited range of types of enquiry – *verificational*. The search is for grounds upon which we may reasonably conclude that this or that argument is valid, this or that proposition true, this or that action right. But those who are seeking such grounds will not all be doing so in the same spirit or for the same purpose, and we need to distinguish different investigations that may be initiated by the use of the same forms of words. One challenger may be satisfied that certain things are true, valid or right, but wish to explore and state the grounds on which his convictions can be firmly based. He may be in the position exemplified by Moore's declaration that he knew for certain that there was chalk on the desk but did not know *how* he knew this, that he could not give a satisfactory philosophical characterisation of the nature and grounds of such knowledge. Another may be in the position of Moore's sceptical opponent: he may think that until an adequate philosophical characterisation of a certain type of knowledge has been given, there is no sufficient ground for claiming to have any knowledge of that type.

The same or a similar distinction may be drawn between

two uses of the question 'What is the *criterion* of truth, or validity, or rightness?' One enquirer may use this form of words in order to raise sceptical questions about whether we *do* know that anything is true or valid or right. Another, though satisfied that he and we have a great deal of knowledge of all these types, may use the same form of words as an invitation to himself and others to try to state explicitly and formally the structural relations between the conclusions expressing such knowledge and the grounds that justify their claim to be instances of knowledge. The distinction we are concerned with here may be compared with the distinction between two people who ask for the statement of a grammatical rule: one may be a foreigner who does not know what the correct grammatical forms are; the other may be a native speaker who is never in doubt about what is the correct thing to say but who has not been able to devise a formula expressing the implicit structure of his impeccable practice.

A frequent and regrettable consequence of confusion between one and another of these distinct enterprises is that philosophers expect general statements of criteria or principles or methods of procedure to achieve what can only be done by attention to the particular and detailed grounds of particular conclusions, whether of fact, or logic, or value. Prichard rightly protests in 'Does Moral Philosophy Rest on a Mistake?' against the uncritical assumption, made by moral philosophers and theorists of knowledge alike, that by formulating a *criterion* they will be able to supply a general statement of the grounds on which this or that whole category of conclusions – moral, factual, logical – may be founded. Two different conclusions, even if they are conclusions of exactly the same type, must have different grounds. What shows that there is a cow in the field is not what shows that there is a horse in the field. The proof that $11 \times 11 = 121$ will not serve as a proof that $12 \times 12 = 144$. Such true remarks as can be made about all arithmetical proofs or all demonstrations of the existence of animals will not characterise, still less constitute, any part of the grounds upon which any particular proposition of arithmetic or any particular existential proposition may be supported.

In discussions of ethics the corresponding delusion is even more prevalent. It expresses itself in aspirations after the formulation of moral principles or criteria by which, it is supposed, particular moral conclusions are to be tested. Even Mill, whose *System of Logic* expounds the view that all reasoning is in the end from particulars to particulars, and that general rules and principles are mere memoranda, tells a different story when he turns from logic and science to ethics. In the second paragraph of *Utilitarianism* he reaffirms the position defended in the *Logic*:

> The truths which are ultimately accepted as the first principles of a science, are really the last results of metaphysical analysis, practised on the elementary notions with which the science is conversant; and their relation to the science is not that of foundations to an edifice, but of roots to a tree, which may perform their office equally well though they be never dug down to and exposed to light.

But in the same paragraph he immediately adds:

> But though in science the particular truths precede the general theory, the contrary might be expected to be the case with a practical art, such as morals or legislation. All action is for the sake of some end, and rules of action, it seems natural to suppose, must take their whole character and colour from the end to which they are subservient. When we engage in a pursuit, a clear and precise conception of what we are pursuing would seem to be the first thing we need, instead of the last we are to look forward to. A test of right and wrong must be the means, one would think, of ascertaining what is right or wrong, and not a consequence of having already ascertained it.

It is against this assumption that Prichard is inveighing

when he warns us that we have no right in advance to expect our obligations to exhibit a neat structure rather than to form an 'unrelated chaos', linked by nothing over and above their being our obligations.

In the same essay Prichard classically draws another distinction that we must attend to if we are to give a satisfactory account of the challenge 'Why should I do what is right?' Such a form of words may be an invitation to offer *inducements* rather than grounds. Prichard alleges that moral philosophers from Plato and Aristotle to the present day have commended morality as profitable to the moral agent. As he points out, such a defence of morality passes by the challenge to offer a direct exposition of the bindingness of moral constraints on rational beings. The connection between morality and prosperity, even if it were universal, would still be indirect. One who pursues for the sake of profit a line of conduct which he takes to be both right and profitable will depart from it if it should turn out, in his opinion, to be right but unprofitable. Its profitability cannot be any part of what makes it right. The same point applies to truth and validity as to moral rightness. To argue that I should believe p, or infer q from p, because it will be to my advantage to do so, is clearly to change the subject from that raised by the epistemological or justificational challenges 'Why should I believe what is true?' and 'Why should I argue validly?' These challenges can be met if at all by the presentation of grounds and not by the offer of inducements.

The parallelisms between the various challenges show again that there is a structure of argument and reason which may be clothed by discourse that is theoretical or practical, logical or factual, descriptive or evaluative. The importance of these distinctions sometimes disguises from us, though we know it well at other times, that logic and reason have a unitary structure in spite of their internal varieties and their manifold applications. This structure will be explained more fully in the next chapter, but it will be convenient to prepare the way into this exploration by summarising some of the relevant results of this and the earlier chapters, and especially by marking the connection between the present topic and our consideration in chapters 3 and 4 of integrity, authenticity and sincerity of action and response.

The mistake made by Hare and the existentialists, of supposing that an authoritative or sovereign reason would compromise human freedom and integrity, may be answered by distinguishing a number of different headings under which a conclusion, whether or not it is a moral conclusion, may relevantly be assessed. If I express a view or make a statement of any kind, it may be appropriate, and will usually be intelligible even when it is not appropriate, to consider any or all of the following questions:

(1) Am I *sincerely* expressing my own conviction or opinion? If not, I may be lying, kowtowing to authority, being polite or complaisant; and no doubt there are numerous other possibilities, but they are all linked by their intelligibility as privations or negations or qualifications of sincerity of expression of what I really believe or feel or know.

(2) Am I *justified* in my assertion or conviction? Am I in possession of adequate grounds for the view that I have expressed? Here again there is great internal variety among the ways in which the answer 'No' may be relevantly supported: I may have attended to misleading data, or reasoned unsoundly from accurate initial information, or committed myself more strongly than the weight of my evidence would warrant; and there are many other possible cases; but again there is a recognisable and distinct heading of assessment.

(3) Am I *right*? Is my conclusion correct or incorrect, true or false, adequate or inadequate to the point and purpose of making a judgement of the kind to which I have committed myself? The terms in which an assessment under this

heading may be conducted and expressed will vary greatly according to whether we are concerned with the validity of a formal argument, the soundness of a statistical generalisation, the legality or morality or utility of an action or an institution, the truth or falsehood of a factual proposition, the acceptability or unacceptability of a theory or interpretation or diagnosis; and each of these sub-headings will have its own variety and internal complexity. (Yet this heading as a whole seems to have a greater unity of structure than any of the others in this list.)

(4) Is it *in my interest* that the matter on which I have expressed a view should be as I have claimed it to be? There is also the related but distinct question: Is it in my interest that it should be *believed*, even if falsely, to be as I have claimed it to be? A few samples will illustrate the variety of cases that may fall under this heading: it may be in my interest that the company's profits should be higher than last year; that a particular financial transaction should be permitted by law; that an action of mine, or of yours, should deserve or be thought to deserve moral praise or condemnation; that a work of art that I own or have created should have or be thought to have a high aesthetic or commercial value; that my child should be or be thought to be beautiful or intelligent or of exemplary moral character.

(5) Do I *want* the right answer to the question to be the answer that I have given? There is again a related but distinct question: Do I want the answer that I have given to be accepted by others? There will naturally be an extensive overlap between this heading and the heading concerned with what is in my interest, and the same list of examples may be used to indicate its scope and variety. But it would be a mistake not to draw a clear distinction between the two headings: I may *want* it to be the case, and/or to be thought to be the case, that *p*, when I falsely believe that the truth of *p*, or its being thought to be true, would be in my interest. It is harder, but not impossible, to produce a case in which

what I rightly believe to be in my interest is something that I hope or wish will not be realised: Captain Oates and others have been known to be determined to sacrifice their own interests to those of others. It is again easy to find and construct examples in which I wish it to be falsely thought that the truth of a proposition is in my interest or not in my interest. I may wish others to believe that it is in my interest that the shares should rise in value, when in fact I am seeking an opportunity to do some cheap buying.

(6) *Why* do I give the answer that I give? I here mean by these words to express a question about what explanation can be given for my answering the question in one way rather than another. The same words often express the question 'What are my *grounds* for the answer that I offer?' That there are certain grounds which appear to me adequate grounds for a certain answer may be the explanation of my giving that answer, but clearly other answers are possible and may be correct even in cases where there *are* good grounds for my answer, and these grounds are available to me. It may be that I am prompted to give and to believe a certain answer because I wish it to be the right answer, and/or the answer accepted by others. I may be influenced by the fact that it is in my interest that the answer I give should be correct, or should be believed by others. It will be seen that almost any item that may be referred to under any of the previous headings may have its place in an explan- ation offered under the present heading. Other ways of summarising this heading, instead of saying that it is concerned with the explanation of the giving of one answer rather than another, would be to say that it is concerned with the causes and motives of the adoption and offering of this or that answer to this or that question.

There are certainly other ways in which answers to questions could be described, classified and assessed. A fuller consideration of this topic would be of philosophical interest in its own right, and would contribute to the clarification of a number of philosophical issues with which we are not here concerned. For the purpose of our present enquiry the partial and summary account that has been given here will be sufficient. It fulfils two main purposes. It is a direct contribution to the description of reasoning in general, and hence both of theoretical and practical reasoning, and it accordingly forms part of the characterisation of moral enquiry that this book is designed to offer. But it also and in particular contributes to the resolution of the conflict between subjective and objective theories, especially in so far as the subjective theories depend on supposed contrasts between theoretical and practical reasoning, or descriptive and evaluative reasoning, in respect of the extent to which passions and sentiments, motives and interests, nature and nurture, environmental and hereditary and other causal influences, determine particular people to give the answers that they give to particular questions.

The first stage of this application to meta-ethics of the list of questions about questions is to point out that every item in the list applies equally to theoretical and practical enquiry, and that therefore no item from it can be made the basis for a differential objection to the objectivity of practical reasoning. Answers to purely theoretical questions also have motives and causes, may arise from interests and desires, may be produced or modified by conditioning (including education, learning and research). If the involvement of any or all of these factors in the production and assessment of answers to any class of questions is a ground for regarding questions of that class as subjective, then it will amount to a ground for regarding as subjective all the questions in the answers to which these same factors are involved; and we should be hard put to it to show that that did not mean all questions whatsoever.

The second stage of the application is to point out that the involvement of such factors in the production and assessment of answers does not show that the questions to which the answers are offered are subjective. The effect of attending to the particular distinctions drawn and illustrated in the list is quite the contrary: it is to make clear the mutual independence of the various factors that are listed, and hence of the various modes of assessment that they exemplify. Sincerity may be combined with truth or with falsehood, with justification or the lack of it. I may have a non-rational motive for believing what is true or for believing what is false. I may be justified or unjustified in believing something that I wish to believe, or something whose truth would be to my advantage. There may be a causal explanation of my believing what is true as well as of my believing what is false. It follows that to give such an explanation of a belief is not *to explain it away*, to show that it is false or ill-founded. Once again it turns out (a) that the sceptic's objection is valid against the objectivity of theoretical enquiry if it is valid against the objectivity of practical enquiry, and (b) that it has no validity against either.

CHAPTER 8

JUSTIFICATION

The necessary emphasis on what is individual and distinctive in morality, and hence in moral scepticism, must not preclude the necessary emphasis on what moral reasoning, as *reasoning*, has in common with other modes of enquiry. In distinguishing the 'interdepartmental difficulties' from the departmental ones we must at the same time remember that they call for answers, even and perhaps especially in a work on moral epistemology, because they are so often confused with the departmental difficulties of ethics, or are thought to present graver obstacles to moral knowledge and understanding than to progress in the various non-moral branches of knowledge. Since in any case moral epistemology, like all epistemology, is a *comparative* study, it will be useful to attend more fully than in the earlier chapters to the place of general epistemological considerations in the task of achieving a just perspective on the nature of moral knowledge.

Without using these specific terms, I have nevertheless been using in this book, and especially in my treatment of the 'is-ought' question, John Wisdom's distinction between 'domestic' logic and 'ultimate' logic (*Paradox and Discovery*, p. 120. See also *Philosophy and Psycho-Analysis*, pp. 280–1). He gives the name of *domestic* logic to the familiar inductive and deductive logic of the text books because it is of the nature of those two species of logic to relate together only propositions

of a given kind and other propositions of that same kind –
members of the same family of propositions. We have seen
that the study of logical relations of this domestic type
cannot provide us with a grasp of the ultimate grounds of a
class of propositions, or indeed of an individual proposition
of any kind. So long as the premises used in support of a
proposition include any propositions of the same type as
itself, a philosophical sceptic, or any other enquirer who is
determined to seek the ultimate grounds, is properly
dissatisfied, since his question is about how propositions
of that whole type are to be validated, and he cannot
consistently permit any such proposition to be unproblematic when it occurs among the premises of an
argument whose conclusion is of the same type.

It is clear that this distinction applies to propositions of all
types, and that to consider it is therefore to deal with one of
the interdepartmental sources of scepticism. Sceptics about
morality, but also about induction, the past and the future,
matter, mind and necessity, all argue more or less explicitly
on the following lines: the grounds offered for a proposition
of kind k will necessarily be either of kind k or not of kind k;
if they are of kind k they may be logically sufficient for the
proposition that they are intended to support, but a further
question will arise about the validation of the premises
themselves; if on the other hand they are not of kind k then
they necessarily cannot be logically sufficient for the truth of
the proposition that they are intended to support.

To emphasise the structural similarity between one
epistemological problem and another, which is exhibited in
the structural similarity between one sceptical argument and
another, might be to be tempted to minimise the differences between the various scepticisms and the objects of
their various sceptical attacks. But to be clear about
the pervasiveness of the unitary structure of the
interdepartmentally sceptical arguments is to be better
equipped to isolate the individual grounds of scepticism

about individual categories of knowledge and understanding, and hence to be better equipped to answer them
by characterising the separate categories one by one.
This can be done for each of them in the manner in which
we have been concerned to do it for moral knowledge and
understanding, and in which, more sketchily, we have
noticed that it can be done for knowledge of other minds.

The task that remains is to show that there are answers to
the interdepartmental objections to the possibility of moral
knowledge, i.e. to those that are offered as objections to the
possibility of knowledge in general, even if they are
mistakenly thought by some philosophers to have unique or
particular force and relevance when they are directed
against the possibility of moral knowledge.

An important first step towards the fulfilment of this task
is to question the traditional and still widespread assumption
that the only or the fundamental way of justifying a
conclusion is to derive it from something that is logically
prior to it. This assumption is a common premise of all
sceptical arguments that express themselves in the form of
requests for the statement of principles or criteria that
knowledge in general or one or more particular kinds of
knowledge must and can satisfy. It is implicit in the
insistence that no *ought* can be supported by an *is*, and in
the corresponding denials offered by sceptics about the
relations between other kinds of knowledge and their
ultimate grounds: sense-experience and material objects,
behavioural premises and psychological conclusions, observed regularities and causal laws, etc. It is also implicit in
the reductive theories that try to answer scepticism by
alleging that in each or any of these cases the ultimate
grounds do or may amount to logically sufficient grounds
for their conclusions.

The assumption is often made explicit, and there are
advantages in facing it directly in its explicit form. Those
who have done so most directly and effectively include C. S.

Peirce, John Stuart Mill and John Wisdom. Peirce remarked
that 'no universal principle is requisite for the validity of any
ordinary inference' (*Values in a Universe of Chance*, p. 164); and
he also noticed that when a philosopher calls something a
'postulate' he is usually thinking of something that is very
well supported by what he calls its consequences. Mill may
have failed to apply his similar insight to ethics, but his
perception of the same point is clear in his *Logic*, and his
formulation shows an awareness that there is no reason to
restrict its application as he does in the opening pages of
Utilitarianism. *All* reasoning, he says, is from particulars to
particulars. Rules and principles, statements of criteria or
conditions for the application of a term or the truth of a
proposition or the justification of a valuation, are valuable if
at all as *memoranda*, as means whereby we bring particulars to
bear upon particulars (*A System of Logic*, II, iii, 4). Wisdom
says that at the bar of reason the final appeal is always to
cases: that examples are the final food of thought (*Paradox
and Discovery*, p. 102). These conclusions are rarely accepted
by philosophers at first sight, and are not often accepted by
philosophers at all.

Wisdom's development of the consequences of these
conclusions is of importance far outside the sphere of moral
philosophy, as the scope of the conclusions themselves would
suggest. Yet there is a twofold advantage for the moral
philosopher to be gained from giving close attention to their
development. We must here again remember that to
characterise reasoning as such is to characterise moral
reasoning among other species of reasoning. As we might
put it in something like Newell's terms, an interdepartmental description is a description of part of each
department. But there is a further and even more powerful
reason for studying the 'case by case' procedure in a book on
ethics, and one that takes the war against moral scepticism
right into the enemy's camp. The sceptic's refrain is that
morality is *different* – different, that is, from logic and fact,

and hence, it is argued or implied, inferior to the very paradigms of rationality. I have not denied that morality is different but I have tried to show that it is not inferior. I have given an account of what the differences are and argued that they are not such as to require us to impugn the rationality of moral reflection. By reference to the account of case by case reasoning that Wisdom is offering, and offering without any special restriction to morality in mind, it becomes possible to reinforce the argument and to present it in a wider epistemological perspective.

A useful first step is to think again of Broad and 'twitting with inconsistency'. The implication of Broad's lugubrious tone was that in ethics we were under limitations from which we were free in science and logic. One of these supposed limitations had to do with the lack of foundations; but another – or perhaps even an alternative way of expressing the same one – was that in ethics we cannot arrive at well founded and authoritative *principles* or *criteria*: that we are condemned to proceed stepwise, piecemeal, case by case. The tables are turned when it is seen that case by case argument is both universal and fundamental. Even in science, even in logic, it is by such a method that we must in the end reason if our reasoning is ultimately to have any cogency. And to argue in such a way is not to be threatened with the Scylla of scepticism or the Charybdis of dogmatism, but to have the best and only sure hope of achieving rationality and objectivity.

The argument for the priority of cases over rules and principles is already prefigured in the distinction between domestic logic and ultimate logic, since the main premise is the recognition that if q follows from p then p cannot be the ultimate ground for q, since one who questions the truth of q and who recognises that q follows from p will also question the truth of p. Wisdom has sometimes put the whole argument into a story whose informality does not disguise the cogency of the strict argument that underlies it.

Suppose that Father, who is a logician, is trying to teach his son the elementary rules of syllogistic reasoning. He writes on the blackboard 'All men are mortal' and 'Socrates is a man', and invites the child to draw a conclusion from these two premises. The boy may be imagined to say that he does not see that any conclusion can be drawn from the premises, and to ask for further explanation. If Father becomes slightly impatient, and insists with some heat that it is possible to conclude from these premises that Socrates is mortal, the child, if he is epistemologically acute, may still ask for *reasons* for accepting the conclusion that he should accept the conclusion. Father is likely at this stage to state a rule or principle to the effect that whenever there are two premises of the form 'All A is B' and '*x* is A' there is sufficient ground for a conclusion of the form '*x* is B'. It is now open to the child to make this further reply:

'Tell me, Father, when you say that *every* instance of an argument of this form is valid, are you including the argument that is written on the blackboard, the argument concerning which we are having this difference of opinion? If you are including it in your statement of the principle, I must point out that your argument is in that case question-begging. You commit the fallacy of *petitio principii* if you argue to a conclusion from a premise which itself contains that conclusion. On the other hand, if you do not mean to include the disputed instance in your statement of your premise, your argument escapes circularity only at the cost of invalidity. For you would then be arguing that since all arguments of this form are valid, except this one, and since this is an argument of this form, therefore this argument is valid; and this argument is a palpable *non sequitur*. I must also point out,' the child may continue, 'that there is a further serious defect in your procedure. Your attempt to convince me that an instance of a certain form of argument is valid is itself an instance of the same form of argument. Once I have denied that it follows from "All men are mortal" and "Socrates is a man" that "Socrates is mortal" you must expect me in all consistency to deny not only any principle from which the validity of this argument logically follows, but also any argument in favour of its validity which, like your present argument, is of the form "All arguments in form F are valid, and this is an argument in form F, therefore this argument is valid." '

You may find this child repellent, but not for his failure to argue correctly. He brings to light something that might more compendiously have been expressed in Descartes's remark that the syllogism belongs more properly to rhetoric than to logic. Once we are convinced that there will be no exceptions we may state our conclusion in the form of an exceptionless rule, but such a rule cannot be the fundamental ground upon which we accept a conclusion about one of its own instances. And when we set out what *is* the fundamental ground it turns out to be in just the form to which the child rightly denies logical cogency, if by logic we mean the formal logic to which the father is confining himself and his son. For it then reads 'Every argument in this form, except this argument, is valid, and therefore this argument is valid' or 'Every other argument in this form is valid, and therefore this argument is valid.' It then gives the fullest grounds we could possibly have for the conclusion about the particular instance before us. Whatever is to provide us with grounds for a conclusion about this instance of an argument in this form must take the form of considering *other* arguments, *other* instances. A rule will not do the work, for a rule cannot refer to the others without referring to this one as well. It does not compete, but simply awards itself the prize. The rule will do only as a piece of rhetoric – as a formulation of the conclusion when we are satisfied that we have reached it or are putting it forward for consideration. It is not the justification of our judgement on the particular instances; on the contrary the particular instances, the character they display when inspected one by one, are the justification for the judgement that the rule is sound.

Wisdom goes on to describe the instruments by which we operate in the dialectical exploration of the manifold of cases, and what he calls the three fundamental operators are naturally reminiscent of the two fundamental operators used and recommended by Leavis: they are 'You might as well say ...' and 'Exactly so' and 'But this is different'. 'You might as well say ...' is the appeal to consistency, as I have repeatedly used it when alleging that the subjectivist about ethics might as well be subjectivist about facts or logic, might as well say that we don't know that the earth is not flat or that we don't know that 12 times 12 is not 99. 'Exactly so' is what the anonymous philosopher says to me in the conversation on pp. 31–2 when he declares that scientific truth is a matter of what is in the end believed by the most respected scientists of our culture circle, and by saying it he concedes too much to be able to preserve his original submission that ethics is subjective and science is not. In order to stay in the ring he must reply to the challenge with an argument to show that 'This is different' – that between ethics and science there is a difference that makes the difference – one that differentiates science as a branch of objective knowledge from ethics as a branch of arbitrary opinion.

When we return to the controversies of moral philosophy, persuaded of these principles, what havoc must we make? We shall at once notice that Hare's main conclusions about moral reasoning are faithfully derived from the initial assumption that to justify a conclusion is to derive it as a logical consequence of something that is prior to it: if I am to justify a moral conclusion, I must therefore have a moral premise, and if that premise in turn is to be supported it must be by reference to a further and prior moral premise. This account of moral argument can only lead to the conclusion that moral reasoning begins with ultimate moral principles for which no reason can be offered or needs to be offered. Though Hare shrinks from calling ultimate moral principles 'arbitrary', there is little but the lack of this word to suggest that in his view they are anything but arbitrarily adopted starting points. Moral reasoning consists in deriving particular moral judgements from such principles, as applied to particular facts, but such a process cannot be represented as the offering of justifications for the judgements that are derived. On Hare's account, as on Hume's, the reason is, and ought only to be, the instrument of purposes in whose adoption it has no place. Such a theory of ethics is sceptical in the strict sense that it denies the coherent possibility of possessing or acquiring *knowledge* of moral truths.

A different and opposed, but equally natural response, when faced with the consequences of applying the traditional prejudice about justification to moral questions, is to substitute dogma for scepticism. Instead of acknowledging that there is no reason for the adoption of the principles that are, according to this view, the fundamental grounds for moral judgements, a philosopher may declare the principles of morality to be intuitively evident: he may describe them as not allowing, but also not requiring, any foundation or justification by reason and argument. He will thus be able to represent morality as objective rather than subjective, but will otherwise differ only in detail from those of his subjectivist opponents who share his assumption about the nature of justification. It is a striking fact, and one that greatly assists us in the preparation of a neutral, non-theoretical description of moral reasoning, that intuitionists like Moore and Ross, and emotivists or prescriptivists like Hare and Stevenson and Ayer and Nowell-Smith, give such closely similar accounts of the process by which a moral dispute moves, through the distinguishing and resolution of questions of fact and logic, to a phase at which all that is at stake is a clash of feelings or commands or intuitions or arbitrary postulates.

The traditional conception of reasoning and justification as exhibiting a hierarchical structure has similar consequences for moral and non-moral judgements alike. In the philosophy of logic, and of perception, and of mind, as in moral philosophy, theories become involved in stark opposition at some points because on other points – and especially on the necessity of a hierarchical or foundational structure of justification – they are closely agreed. And the argument for such a structure, though it amounts to little more than the assumption that there must be such a structure – to the imposition of what Wittgenstein called a *requirement* – is highly persuasive. It embodies a picture that easily fascinates and captivates the mind. A conclusion surely needs a reason to support it. But every reason is itself a conclusion and therefore needs a further reason in its own support. Unless we can call a halt at some point we seem to be threatened with an infinite regress. The sceptic denies that we can ever call a halt, and takes the upshot to be that knowledge and justification are necessarily impossible. They require the fulfilment of conditions that necessarily cannot be fulfilled. The conventionalist says 'Let us call a halt. There is a point beyond which reasoning cannot go on, a point where we must and do simply adopt certain principles.' The intuitionist says that we can call a halt because we can arrive at self-evident principles or intuitively evident judgements on particular cases which cannot be argued about but are known to be correct, and which can serve as the foundations and grounds of the remainder of our knowledge, of all the knowledge that requires validation by the provision of reasons or evidence.

This language is all familiar from the debates and disputes of moral philosophers, but it is equally at home in other philosophical conflicts. For if the hierarchical structure has any application at all it will apply to the principles of logic themselves, and hence to all enquiry in which logical reasoning is required, and hence to *all* enquiry. Since the time of Aristotle it has been argued that the ultimate principles of logic must simply be accepted as self-evident or arbitrarily adopted. You cannot argue *by* the principles of logic *for* the principles of logic without circularity or regress. Their validity must be recognised or assumed as a basis for the establishment of other truths, including other truths of logic.

The intuitionist and the adoptionist agree on a point that is at least as fundamental as anything on which they disagree. They both endorse the maxim *de principiis non est disputandum*. It is here that they make their fundamental error. If we are to escape from the mazes and dilemmas of traditional epistemology, whether in its general form or in its specifically moral variant, we must follow the arrow that points upwards to the top of the blackboard from the particulars to the principles, and not the arrow of deductive logic that points downwards from the so-called axioms or principles to the particulars. To escape from the sceptical implications of the standard assumptions about proof and explanation, meaning and justification, we need to recognise that the question 'are all things of this *sort* good or bad?' cannot be answered by somebody who does not know the answer to any question of the form 'is *this* thing good or bad?' We must abandon the idea that to justify a moral or any other conclusion about an instance of an action or person or character or motive is to apply to that instance a principle from which, together with a description of the instance, the conclusion about the instance logically follows. If the question 'is *this* x good?' has not been answered, then the question 'are *all* xs good?' has not been answered. The mistake that philosophers have made in ethics is the mistake that they have made in all other branches of epistemology: they think that the foundations of our knowledge are to be looked for in the sky and not in the soil.

When Wittgenstein urged us to look back at the process of teaching he pointed in the right direction. The ultimate appeal for or against anything that is offered to us as an addition to our knowledge is to something that we have learned before. There can be no justification for any conclusion if there is no appeal to what we have learned before, and in the end, in ethics as elsewhere, the appeal is to how we learned to think and speak in the first place. If we can build high structures of scientific or logical or moral or any other kind of knowledge, we can build them only on the ground on which we stand. Unless we can understand and know what is primitive and unproblematic we cannot have any confidence in the safety of taller and more complex structures.

This way of speaking, though deliberately chosen to repudiate the foundation picture, may restore it in another form unless some further explanation is given. The idea that common sense and common language, what we learn at mother's knee, provides solid ground on which we can then build the rest of our knowledge, may point its epistemological arrows in the right direction, and rightly set the sky above the soil, but it still incorporates the contrast between the evident and the problematic, the secure starting point and the fragile finished product, that causes most of the confusion that arises from the traditional analogies. Both the danger and the cure for it can be seen for what they are if we notice how natural it is to ask *how* we know that the ground is solid, that the particular instances have the character we attribute to them when we look back to what we learned at mother's knee. This question often attracts the answer that is also often given to the corresponding question raised about first principles when they are conceived as axioms or postulates or ultimate premises from which the rest of our knowledge is derived by deduction: it is natural to answer 'By *intuition*'.

Wittgenstein said that intuition was 'an unnecessary shuffle'. He was thinking of logic and mathematics, but his remark has a wider application because the same structure repeats itself from one epistemological context to another. Wittgenstein presumably meant that nothing of substance is achieved by the answer, since it differs only in form from saying that we know the fundamentals of our knowledge without having any reasons on the basis of which we know them. The question 'How do you know?' seems to presuppose that there will be an answer in terms of a procedure, technique, faculty or method – something of which we can say that it is by operating it or applying it or following it or consulting its deliverances that we establish our elementary knowledge and understanding. The question is misconceived if it is construed like this. There is no such faculty or method or procedure. To say that we know intuitively is just to say that we know, and to pretend to describe or explain how we know.

It is to be expected that the sceptic will protest at this point. Whether we speak of intuition or of just knowing without any basis or faculty or procedure, are we not in either case confessing that we do not really *know*, that we are granting ourselves the credit of this honorific title without authority? Are we not confessing, openly or by evasion, that we cannot produce the title deeds, that we have no *reason* for our claim? And this is what the sceptic had been alleging from the start.

The challenge can be turned against itself. The sceptic purports to be offering reasons for his scepticism, reasons for saying that our conclusions *are not justified*. Unless he is using the word 'justification' as we also use it, his denial can have no relevance to our assertion. This is the point that Wittgenstein makes when he says that 'this is what we *call* a justification here.' Wittgenstein is including the sceptic among those referred to by 'we': like all of us, he recognises what counts as a justification, and if he did not he could not intelligibly controvert our claim to give one in this or that case or type of case. He can deny that what we offer as a justification is a justification, and in that sense he can correctly say 'That may be what you call a justification, but it is not what I call a justification.' But those words cannot be allowed to suggest that he does not share our *concept* of justification, that he has something altogether different in mind whenever he uses the word 'justification', since he would not in that case be denying that we have offered a *justification*, but denying that we have offered something else that for good or bad reasons he happens to call by the same name. The source of his understanding of the notion of justification is the same as the source of ours. There must therefore be cases that he will call cases of justification and that we shall also call cases of justification, and this means that he and we can 'twit each other with inconsistency' in a process of comparison and contrast of cases that is the form that reasoning takes in such a conflict. In this space as in other spaces we can locate ourselves and each other, and can dispute the locations of things, only if there are things whose locations are not disputed. We shall then find that reflective collaboration, even if it takes the form of disputation, will ensure that the locations of some things whose locations we at first disputed will at last cease to be disputed.

The analogy with spatial location that is implicit in some of these remarks deserves to be made explicit. We cannot dispute with each other or ask each other about or help each other with the location of an object in space unless we are both oriented in the space about which we disagree or about which one of us needs the help of the other. To be oriented is to know the position of some objects in space and so to be able to use them as points of reference for the location of others. We may use maps or guidebooks, but these devices are not fundamental: they depend on the epistemologically prior procedure of relating point to point in the space. There are many direct analogies between the exploration of space and the exploration of *logical* space.

The exploration of either space is inexhaustible. There is no end to the possibilities of specifying the spatial relations between objects in physical space or the logical relations between descriptions of instances in logical space. When we consider this feature of enquiry in general, especially if we do so under the influence of a sceptical philosopher, we can easily be tempted to construe the endlessness and openness of the process as necessarily involving *inconclusiveness*, as making it impossible to arrive at any firm truth or knowledge. But the temptation is weakened when we remember that the inexhaustibility of the exploration of physical space, the fact that there is no end to the possibilities of specifying the spatial relations between a particular object and other objects in the same space, does not make it impossible for us ever to know where we are.

An enquiry may be inexhaustible without being in-conclusive. It may be possible to go further and still not be necessary to go further. I may conclude that addition of integers is commutative without having, *per impossibile*, examined every pair of integers. The doctor may diagnose the growth as malignant after examining it for a finite time and without looking at it from the infinitely many angles from which it is visible. It is a lesson of experience that too many cooks spoil the broth even if more experience may teach us the same lesson again. In fact it can be a correct lesson only if further experience *will* teach the same lesson again. We may have all the reason we need without having all the reason we could have for any one of these conclusions or for any other conclusion. There is always something for the sceptic to say, and always something to say to him in reply. We must not be deceived, as he is, into thinking that because the debate continues our case is lost. The twitting never has to stop but there may be no need for it to go on.

The sceptic's perception and misconstruction of the significance of the endlessness of enquiry can be exposed as clearly as anywhere in his understanding and mis-understanding of logical validity. He is dissatisfied with a case by case proof of the soundness of an argument because it leaves open the possibility of further enquiry into the soundness of that argument. And the possibility of further enquiry remains open as long as there are unexamined cases, and there are always unexamined cases. But he is equally dissatisfied with a deductive proof, from a rule or principle, of the validity of an argument, and asks for the authority and credentials of the rule or principle. The principle is itself to the effect that all cases of a certain sort answer to a certain other description, and so itself involves for its validity exactly the same inexhaustible and incompletable examination of cases that the proof by cases requires.

The same impasse can be illustrated in all the contexts, including this one, where Wisdom's contrast between domestic and ultimate logic has application. The efficient sceptic must reject any attempt to derive the moral from the moral, the material from the material, the mental from the mental, either by deductive or by any non-deductive procedure. A deductive derivation will be *from* the moral, the material, the mental: it proves too much. A non-deductive procedure is invalid because it is not a derivation *from* the moral, the material, the mental: it proves too little.

This is the familiar region in which we find the gulf between *is* and *ought*, the impassable barrier between description and evaluation − including, as I have argued, description of the form of an argument and evaluation of the argument as sound. To ascribe form *F* to the argument is merely to describe it, and must be merely to describe it if it is to be the ultimate justification of the claim that the argument is valid. But since it merely describes it cannot validate, evaluate, justify the desired conclusion. The ascription of form is not good enough. The direct ascription of validity is too much. Everything we offer and everything we could conceivably offer is either too little or too much. Nothing will ever do.

Nothing will ever do to meet the sceptic's requirement. But that is different from saying that nothing will ever do. There are no canonical starting points − no such *archai* or *principia* as are envisaged by the traditional picture of justification – but we do not need them. If we reject the traditional picture we can agree with the sceptic about the inexhaustibility of enquiry and still repudiate his scepticism. Any conclusion, any judgement on any particular case, and *a fortiori* any more general judgement or rule or principle, can at any stage or at any time be rationally questioned and criticised. This follows directly from the inexhaustibility of the proof of any conclusion, but its significance for the answering of scepticism will be plainer if it is expressed through the analogy with spatial location. A landmark is itself an object in space. Its use as a landmark is *ad hoc*, and on other occasions it may be the very object into whose location we or others are enquiring. Nothing could fulfil the role of a landmark without being in the space in which it is used to give us our bearings, and nothing can be in that space without being capable of being located with reference to other objects in that space. And this is little if anything more than an indirect way of stating the familiar and unexciting conclusion that space is relative and not absolute. There are no privileged locations.

The idea of the relativity of logical space causes more excitement. Both the sceptic and his dogmatist opponent assume that the absoluteness of logical space is necessary for the objectivity of enquiry; that in seeking knowledge and understanding we orient ourselves, if at all, by fixed landmarks whose own positions neither can be nor need to be the subject of investigation. Sceptics become sceptical because they recognise that what they believe to be necessary is nevertheless not possible. Dogmatists become dogmatic because they rebel against the paradoxes of scepticism but still agree with the sceptics on what is necessary for the validity of our knowledge. One party denies the possibility of knowledge because it sees that logical space is relative and the other denies that logical space is relative because it sees that knowledge is possible. Hence the unceasing round of assertions and denials of the availability and efficacy of intuitions, first principles, foundations – a turmoil that can be stilled only by insisting that what is not possible is also not necessary.

It is not possible to inspect every actual and possible instance of S in order to establish that all S is P, and the sceptic will therefore say that we can never have all the reason that we could have, and hence never all the reason that we need, for concluding that all S is P. But since he is right in saying that we cannot inspect every instance and wrong in saying that we can never know the conclusion he must be wrong in supposing that we cannot justify the conclusion without examining every instance. In general: since he is right in supposing that we can never take into account every consideration relevant to the truth or falsehood of any conclusion, and wrong in supposing that we can never know what is true and what is false, he must be wrong in supposing that I can never know the truth or falsehood of a conclusion without having taken into account everything that is relevant to the question of its truth or falsehood. You might as well say that I cannot know where the Eiffel Tower is because there are spatial relations between it and other objects in space that I have never considered and shall never consider and have no intention of ever trying to consider.

The endlessness of space is a good reason for holding that we shall never come to the end of space but no reason for supposing that we shall never make a move in space. We cannot count all the natural numbers but we can count indefinitely many of the natural numbers. We cannot know everything that is knowable but that is no reason for supposing that we cannot know indefinitely many of the things that are knowable.

But there *is* good reason to conclude that enquiry and debate are potentially endless, and that nothing is the unalterable and immovable base on which any party to any conflict is condemned to stand with his back to the wall and with nowhere to turn for further explanation and defence. The old slogan *de principiis non est disputandum* turns out to be mistaken even when we rightly understand what are the *principia*, the origins or starting points of our knowledge and understanding. It is doubly wrong when it is read as referring to *archai* or *principia* in the sense of the traditional structure of justification. There is no inescapable end to any disputation. There is always another argument, always another case to bring to bear, another comparison or contrast to draw and defend or dismiss. This openness and endlessness is so far from having the implications that moral sceptics seek to draw from it that it can be used in the refutation of their scepticism.

For I am not only recommending and describing a method: I am also directly employing it. I am saying to the sceptic about morality 'You might as well be sceptical about logic. You might as well say that we can never know an argument to be valid.' To this challenge – 'You might as well say' – he may again respond in either of two different ways. The moral sceptic may respond by saying 'Exactly so', and thus reveal himself as just a *sceptic* (full stop) – one who is sceptical always and everywhere. If so, he is to be dealt with more fully on another occasion, though much that has been said on this occasion is still addressed to him. The alternative response, and one that is more common in debates about moral philosophy, is to declare that *this is different*, that logical validation is not like moral valuation, and is unlike it in respects that are relevant to the conclusion that one of them is objectively rational and the other not.

In replying to this challenge I have used the same procedure again. I have argued that no relevant distinction has been shown or can be shown between the conclusion that an argument is good and the conclusion that a character or an action is good. In both cases we are concerned with valuation, and with what a man commits himself to by what he says. We can hold that there is an impassable gulf between an *is* and a moral *ought* only if we also hold that there is an impassable gulf between an *is* and a logical *ought*, between the description of the form of a valid argument and the endorsement of the argument as sound. Or we can reject this perverse account of logic, can recognise that the description of the character of an argument, free from terms of explicit logical appraisal, *is* what shows it to be a sound or an unsound argument; and then we can no longer draw from this source any reason for scepticism about morals.

The sense in which, in Hume's phrase, morality rests upon 'the particular fabric and constitution of the human species' is paralleled by a sense in which logic also rests upon the particular fabric and constitution of the human species. Logic is not rendered subjective by this dependence, and morality is not rendered subjective by the corresponding dependence. For the dependence is not a dependence of the truths of logic or of morality upon facts about human beings. It is rather that the intelligibility to us of both agreement and conflict, both in logic and in morality, depends on our sharing a set of responses, upon our reacting in closely similar ways.

CHAPTER 9

REASON

Yossarian's respectful reply to the psychiatrist's question was formulated in such a way as to allow us to answer 'Both': to say that Colonel Ferredge finds Yossarian's dream disgusting because there is some quality in the dream and some quality in Colonel Ferredge (see p. 1). Butler sees morality as founded upon a faculty that may be described both as a sentiment of the understanding and as a perception of the heart. We are not forced to give an account of moral choice and action either exclusively in terms of 'argument and induction' or wholly in terms of 'feeling and internal sense'. There is a place in morality and moral philosophy for attention to 'the particular fabric and constitution of the human species', but also a place for reason and argument. And Butler's *Sermons* and Dissertation illustrate and demonstrate that due attention to our particular fabric and constitution will itself lead us to recognise the place of reason in ethics. We are rational animals, creatures composite of mind and body, and our thoughts as well as our feelings must be given the scope in any portrayal of our human nature that they actually claim for themselves in the daily detail of our human lives.

We saw that Butler himself was following Aristotle when he spoke of the unity of sentiment and perception, heart and understanding. Aristotle's concepts of rational appetite and appetitive reason are his expression of the union of reason and emotion in action and choice. A choice – a *proairesis* – the origination of a human action, may be called either *orexis dianoetikē* or *orektikos nous* because it is a unity, a union of understanding and desire, and because neither the understanding nor the desire is to be given precedence over the desire or the understanding in the apprehension and description of the unity (*Nicomachean Ethics*, 1139b4–5). Whether we put the reason into the adjective or into the noun, the desire into the noun or into the adjective, will vary with the direction from which on a particular occasion we view or approach the composite of *understanding-and-being-moved* that is a choice. And that is the kind of originator of change that a man is – *kai hē toiautē archē anthrōpos*. It is in the nature of the beast to be an indissoluble compound of reason and desire, and it is in his capacity as such a compound that a human being changes the world.

In the same context Aristotle uses a phrase that has given rise to one of the slogans of moral subjectivism : *dianoia outhen kinei*. In the form of the Latin tag, *intellectus nihil movet*, it has repeatedly been used to express an endorsement of Hume's side in the Hume/Kant controversy about feeling and reason. It is a pity that those who have used it for this purpose have not taken seriously the whole sentence in which it occurs: *dianoia d'autē outhen kinei, all'hē heneka tou kai praktikē* (1139a35). The verb in effect occurs twice in the sentence, and though on the first occurrence it is negated by *outhen*, on its implied second occurrence it has positive force. What may easily be missed, and must be missed by any reader who wishes to use Aristotle's words in support of Hume, is that the subject of the verb in both occurrences is *dianoia*. A paraphrase that would bring out these points clearly might be : 'The understanding itself moves nothing – the unqualified understanding; it causes movement only if it is a purposive, practical understanding – one that aims at an end'.

It may be added in defence and explanation of Aristotle,

and of Butler who follows him so closely in this and other respects, that they too, just as much as Hume, are concerned with humanity. In fact their concern with humanity is more comprehensive than that of Hume, for whom the intellect 'is and ought only to be the slave of the passions.' The life of a man as Aristotle sees it is *zoē praktikē tis tou logon echontos* (1146a8). A life that does not involve practical activities is not the life of or the life appropriate to a human being. The life of man adds to the functions of vegetable and animal life a distinctively human faculty of understanding which is capable of being applied in action as well as of being employed in pure contemplation. That is why there is need and scope for the virtue of *phronēsis*. For *phronēsis* is both an intellectual grasp and understanding – it is excellence in the use of the *dianoia heneka tou kai praktikē* of 1139a35 – and a capacity for and a disposition towards various modes of action and activity. The *phronimos* is *praktikos* (1146a8). Knowledge is necessary but not sufficient for the attribution of *phronēsis*; action in accordance with the relevant knowledge is also necessary: *ou tōi eidenai monon phronimos alla kai tōi praktikos* (1152a9).

It will be clear how close is the kinship between the argument of this book and the central conceptions of Aristotle's moral philosophy. The connections are close enough to permit a general account of Aristotle's *phronēsis* to serve also as a statement of the main conclusions of this work. This procedure will involve us in some questions of Aristotelian interpretation, but the points of interpretation are so intimately linked with points of philosophical substance that to consider them is at the same time to take part in the direct discussion of the philosophical issues.

The main issue is about the nature of the connection between *phronēsis* and action. How can the possession of *phronēsis*, of any form of understanding, *guarantee* the performance of the appropriate action? The most valuable clue is provided by the equation of *orektikos nous* and *dianoētikē orexis* with *proairesis*; for this equation makes clear that the relation between *phronēsis* and action is not a causal but a logical relation. To say that the *phronimos* is *praktikos* (1146a8), or that *eti ou tōi eidenai monon phronimos alla kai tōi praktikos* (1152a9), is not to say that 'experience shows' that the man in possession of *phronēsis* will in fact do what is right. It is to say that the man who does not do what is right cannot be allowed to count as *phronimos*.

Once again a comparison with theoretical reasoning helps to clarify the point. If I can rightly claim to see the validity of an argument whose premises I accept, then I shall accept the conclusion of the argument; and the connection here again is logical and not causal. One who does not accept the conclusion of a valid argument whose premises he accepts is not qualified to be described as recognising the validity of the argument. Nor is it sufficient that he should go through the external motions of accepting the conclusion. He must be *convinced* of the truth of the conclusion, he must *accept* it as a datum for any further relevant action or reflection.

There is controversy among philosophers about this parallel, and to enter into the dispute is to come to the heart of what I want to say about the relation between theory and practice. Those whom I have been calling moral sceptics are in the habit of asking in a challenging manner 'How can an *action* be the conclusion of an argument?' Surely, it is argued, the conclusion of an argument must be a *proposition*, since the purpose of an argument is to establish the *truth* of its conclusion; even when we use *reductio ad absurdum* arguments, we are still concerned to pass from and to what is true-or-false. Actions do not have truth-values, they cannot appropriately be assessed as either true or false.

The same point is made about feelings and emotions. How can a man be *argued* into hope or fear or hate or love? The understanding moves nothing – *intellectus nihil movet* – and hence it does not move the heart any more than it moves the limbs.

We face here a typical philosophical situation in which two opposed mistakes are engaged in a conflict that is all the more persistent and intense for being based on a third mistake that is made by both the conflicting parties. One party conceives reason as purely theoretical, and altogether excludes it from the sphere of the practical, from the world of feeling, emotion and action, except as a 'slave to the passions', an instrument for the pursuit of ends in whose choice or foundation it necessarily has no place. These are the thinkers of the post-Kantian coalition in which emotivists and prescriptivists have made common cause with existentialists, moral sceptics and irrationalists who, whatever their differences on other points, all regard reasoning in ethics as being concerned only with means and not with the choice of ends.

To every philosophical reaction there is an equal and opposite over-reaction. In opposition to those who derationalise ethics it has been common to over-intellectualise morality in order to secure its place within the sphere of reason. Socrates is under reasonable suspicion of this mistake, and Plato escapes condemnation, if at all, only because his conception of the structure of the human mind and character, when combined with his account of the methods and purposes of dialectic, so heavily qualifies the initial misunderstanding that his Socratic formulae – 'virtue is knowledge', 'no man does wrong willingly', would otherwise seem to express.

The mistake from which both these misrepresentations directly arise is a determination to affirm the unity of reason even at the cost of denying the multiplicity of its modes. Reason is unified by being confined to its purely theoretical employment. For the use of the reason as a mere *instrument* of practice – as a slave of the passions – is still strictly theoretical in its process and in its results, since its deliverances are to the effect that such and such a consequence will or may follow from such and such an action. Aristotle's chief contribution to ethics – and one that is fully characteristic of his philosophical method and manner in any department of the subject – was to diagnose and treat the source of this mistake.

Aristotle's treatment of reason is an application of his recognition that epistemic terms such as *nous* and *epistēmē* are analogical and not univocal or equivocal. The cross-connections and distinctions to which he thus contrives to do equal justice may be illustrated in a simple diagram:

theoretical	practical
assertion	pursuit
denial	avoidance

Assertion and denial are both 'propositional attitudes' or 'propositional acts', though of opposite tendency, and they therefore appear in the same column but in different rows. Pursuit and avoidance are non-propositional, practical acts, and correspondingly each must appear in the same column as the other but in a different row. But is there any reason why assertion and pursuit should appear together in one row and denial and avoidance should be put together, though in another and different row? If theoretical and practical reason were both called 'reason' by a sheer equivocation, there would be no basis on which entries in the theoretical and practical rows in the diagram could be correlated, and there would accordingly be no particular reason for having a single diagram instead of two separate lists, one for theoretical reason and one for practical reason. In my diagram the rows would in that case have no significance comparable with the clear point of the columns.

Since the rows do clearly have an independent significance, the diagram illustrates a systematic connection between theoretical reason and practical reason, as may be made explicit by adding to the diagram some suitable signs or words to indicate what is common to the pairs of terms that appear in the same row:

	theoretical	*practical*
Yes	assertion	pursuit
No	denial	avoidance

Platonists erase the line between the theoretical and the practical. The subjectivist or imperativist incises the line so deeply that he makes the two columns into two separate lists whose spatial proximity expresses no conceptual parallel.

The greater part of the rest of Aristotle's moral philosophy flows from his initial insight into the analogical connection between the columns. When he says that we become good not by nature alone or by training alone, but by a combination of nature and training, he is thinking as much of the education of the emotions as of the training of the theoretical intelligence. In the sphere of practice, as in that of theoretical learning, we begin by possessing *dunameis tōn enantiōn* – capacities for opposites. We need to be shaped and guided into the appropriate *hexeis*, states of mind and character whose expression will consist in acting and feeling rightly as well as in being able to say how it is appropriate to feel and to act.

Aristotle accordingly uses two different but related ways of specifying the sphere of application of the moral virtues and vices. Moral assessment is relevant both to pleasures and pains and to actions and passions. By 'passions' here Aristotle means, as the Greek word '*pathē*' often does, not only or primarily the passions in the sense of internal states or agitations such as those of anger, fear or love, but any passive state or condition, any undergoing or being the object of an action or occurrence. The same idea is used in the famous sentence in the *Poetics* in which Aristotle contrasts poetry with history. The poet deals with what is universal, the historian with the particular, such as what Alcibiades did or what happened to Alcibiades (*ti Alkibiades epraxen ē ti epathen*, 1451b11). The phrase covers the whole biography of Alcibiades, and hence the usual translation ('what Alcibiades did or suffered') may mislead the English reader into understanding its scope too narrowly.

The two ways of specifying the sphere of the virtues and vices are connected by Aristotle's remark at 1104b14 that every action and passion is accompanied by pleasure or pain. He makes clear that the pleasures and pains as well as the actions and 'passions' are proper objects of moral approbation and disapprobation. Some of the consequences of Aristotle's account seem highly paradoxical if they are not put in their proper relation to his conception of the connection and distinction between practical reason and theoretical understanding.

The man who is *phronimos* combines an *alēthēs logos* with an *orexis orthē*: he has both a right reason or understanding and a right desire, and is therefore armed on two fronts against the complaint of Heraclitus that men live as though they had private or individual understanding of the *logos*: *tou logou eontos xunou zōousin hoi polloi hōs idian echontes phronēsin*. An *orthos logos* is common, public, not variable according to the wish or whim of the individual who may be applying it in a given case. If my case is different it will call for a different judgement, but still for a judgement in accordance with right reason. The relativities that must be taken into account in comparing case with case do not compromise the rationality and objectivity of the judgements on the cases. A tailor who does not relate the cut and size of a coat to the individuality of his client will not serve the client well. No cut or size of coat will suit both Bismarck and the poet, or, except by rare coincidence, any two different men. But this does not invalidate the tailor's skill: it is precisely what calls for its careful application.

When Aristotle makes his contrast between things that are 'pleasant by nature' and those which give pleasure to a corrupted human nature, but are not objectively pleasant, the modern reader does not need to be committed to an explicit moral philosophy in order to feel that he is being asked to stomach an indigestible paradox. Aristotle frequently adds an illustration which may seem to do little to soften the paradox. The good man is the standard and measure of what is pleasant or painful in the way that the healthy man is the standard and measure of what is sweet or bitter, and in general of what are literally matters of taste (1113a25–b1).

There may be something quaint in Aristotle's way of expressing his conclusion, especially when it is viewed through the idioms of a language that is not his own, but the substance of his moral teaching is here as in most places quite close to what we ordinarily recognise for ourselves when we are not engaged in philosophical examination of our common understanding. We do recognise that some things are, and other things are not, proper objects of enjoyment. We recognise that there is something wrong with a man if he enjoys suffering pain or enjoys inflicting pain. We regard these tendencies as unnatural and abnormal; we should feel the need for a special explanation of their occurrence as we should not of a liking for flowers or an interest in music.

These last examples already show that Aristotle's point applies outside the range of bodily pleasures and pains in the narrowest sense of those phrases. Its range of application is even wider than these examples indicate. There are clear if not always sharp distinctions between what it is natural and reasonable to find frightening, or exciting or surprising or puzzling or amusing, and what will frighten, excite, surprise or puzzle only a man who either has not understood the situation or is oversensitive or insensitive to some aspect or feature of it.

The Aristotelian *phronimos* or *spoudaios* is the morally healthy person who enjoys doing what is right. Aristotle repeatedly insists that merely doing what is right is not enough; we must be or become the sort of men who naturally and therefore without inner strain and therefore pleasurably and without distress do what is right. A simple example can illustrate his conception and at the same time show how close it is to that of 'the ordinary moral consciousness.' If you give up your seat on the train to an overburdened young mother, and I give up mine to a frail old man, we may both make our sacrifices with an impeccable outward grace, even though my inner state of agitation and reluctance is hard for me to disguise, while your good nature and practised generosity make your action effortless and painless. If somebody now asks, 'Which is the more meritorious?' we are drawn in opposite ways. My action costs me more, is more of an achievement than yours; I have overcome an obstacle, even if only an internal obstacle. But you show yourself the better man; you have already achieved the state of character towards which I am at the best still aspiring and striving.

The conflict is resolved when we take seriously the idea of moral training, learning and education. We praise a young child for executing with difficulty an exercise that an older child can carry out with ease without receiving or deserving any particular credit. Some schools award prizes for effort as well as for achievement, and the prizes for effort do not usually go to those whose achievements are the most impressive. Some praise and some rewards are designed as encouragements to those who are still acquiring skills and accomplishments. We also praise and prize the acquired skill and its products, and the native talent that is fulfilled when it is acquired and exercised. The different species or senses of praise and reward have different objects and different ends, and there is no paradox or contradiction in the fact that they may be assigned to different people or qualities or actions in the same context. If we hold a competition or examination for children of widely differing ages we shall arrange the children in age groups, and take their ages as well as their scores into account in awarding prizes or marks of merit. If the oldest and the youngest competitors produce identical performances, the achievement of the youngest child is more meritorious, and the recognition of it as such does not conflict with the recognition of the absolute values of the two scores as identical.

The parallelism that Aristotle sees between theoretical and practical reasoning is further displayed in his conception of 'the intellectual virtues.' Modern ethical theorists who have fixed a gulf between reason and practice have accordingly paid little or no attention to the qualities that Aristotle refers to as *dianoētikai aretai*. A minor but not a negligible cause of this neglect is the quaintness to modern ears of the expression 'intellectual virtue', and the lack of any natural and customary equivalent phrase. But it is not difficult to identify in plain modern English the qualities of mind that Aristotle and many other philosophical moralists have set beside the qualities of character that are still sometimes called 'moral virtues' as elements in the nature and description of the good man. Other things being equal, a man who is wise or intelligent or ingenious or far-seeing is more admirable than one who is foolish, stupid, slow-witted or short-sighted, even in contexts where these terms lack the moral connotations that they often bear. We value knowledge, and the intellectual gifts that promote the acquisition of knowledge, even when we have no ulterior practical or moral motive for doing so.

But the purely theoretical employment of the intellectual virtues does not exhaust their use and value. The distinction between reason and feeling, intellect and emotion, is a different distinction from that between the theoretical and practical, and it does not even run parallel to it, as it is required to do by some of the familiar moral theories that it is my purpose to controvert.

Aristotle's ethical theory has lessons to teach to a generation in which many philosophers have exaggerated the difference between theoretical and practical reasoning to the point of denying that practical reasoning is really reasoning. They are all the more valuable because they are combined with the lessons he teaches to Platonists of his own or any generation who exaggerate the kinship between theoretical and practical reasoning to the point of asserting or implying that practical reasoning is really theoretical. His account is implicitly based on the denial of the mistaken assumption which is common to two otherwise mutually opposed accounts of morality: the assumption that all reasoning is theoretical. Plato recognises that there is rationality in morals and therefore represents morality as more theoretical than it is. The modern 'prescriptivist' or subjectivist or emotivist recognises that moral rationality is very different from any purely theoretical rationality and therefore denies that it is a species of rationality at all, or confines it to the role assigned to it by Hume when he said that 'reason is and ought only to be the slave of the passions'. Neither inference is plausible to one who denies their common premise that reasoning is necessarily a purely theoretical process.

Aristotle's corrective to Plato necessarily involves a reconsideration of the problem of *akrasia* and of the Socratic paradox that all wrongdoing is involuntary, since this problem is the decisive test case for an account of the relation between reason and feeling, judgement and action. It is the phenomenon of *akrasia*, with its revelation of the practicality of practical reason, that is held by one group of those to whom my account is opposed to show that there is a logical gulf between practical reason and theoretical reason; and it is the same phenomenon that prompts the other group of those to whom my account is opposed to tighten up the requirements for rationality to a point where nothing practical can count as rational, and even practice has to be intellectualised before it can call for the application of the intellect. *Akrasia* requires for its correct description and explanation an account that gives due recognition to the kinship as well as to the recognised difference, the distinction as well as the recognised kinship, between theoretical and practical thinking.

One step towards such an account is to attend to an *unrecognised* kinship between theory and practice. This kinship already begins to be visible in the parallels between approval and belief and between goodness and truth (see pp. 21–2). The kinship is a consequence or manifestation of the fact that it is *human beings* who think theoretical thoughts and arrive at theoretical conclusions, just as it is human beings who think practical thoughts and feel emotions that move them to arrive at practical conclusions. We need to give a wider range of application than is commonly given to the slogan that the intellect moves nothing. It is not only pursuit and avoidance that are movements, responses, reactions of the composite organism: assertion and denial are also *actions*, and belief and disbelief, confidence, doubt, faith and hope, even if they are not all properly called emotions, are at any rate all *attitudes*, which are often, in the older text books of logic, psychology and epistemology, called 'propositional attitudes'. It is not fair to the humanity of the activity of enquiry, when comparing it with other human actions and activities, to treat it as a bloodless abstraction while representing *praxis* and the practical life with all the blood still circulating in their veins.

There is a close connection between the paradoxes of Socrates and the insight that Hume expresses in the first Appendix to the *Enquiry Concerning the Principles of Morals*: 'But after every circumstance, every relation is known, the understanding has no further room to operate, nor any object on which it could employ itself.' The connection is partly hidden by the fact that Hume is usually quoted in connection with moral conflict between one man and another, while Socrates is concerned with inner conflict. But this is a superficial difference, not only in this context but in general. For whenever I am halting between two opinions it is possible to imagine the same two opinions as those of two distinct individuals or parties; and whenever I take part in or observe a conflict between two parties or two individuals, I can envisage a conflict along the same lines occurring as an inner conflict. What Socrates and Hume are showing if not saying is that a moral conflict cannot occur between two individuals or parties, or between two sides or elements within an individual, unless one side's apprehension differs from that of the other side.

When we look at moral conflict as we know it, we find that it does not end in deadlock because it does not end at all. We may become tired or impatient, and give up the struggle with others or with ourselves, but we do not at such times think that there is nothing more to be said, but only that nothing is to be gained by saying it; we do not conclude that there are no circumstances and relations that could relevantly be drawn to the attention of the people with whom we are at odds – and they may again be ourselves – but we know or suspect or mistakenly believe that they are too blind or stupid or stubborn or self-interested or dogmatic or emotional to see the bearing of those facts and circumstances. And that list of moral and intellectual failings is a list of the failings that also keep us from thinking and seeing straight in non-moral contexts, both in theory and in practice. That is why Socrates asked us to learn and exercise the moral and intellectual virtues that are equal and opposite to these failings: self-knowledge, self-criticism, clarity, consistency, patience, the faith and the courage to follow the argument where it leads.

BIBLIOGRAPHY

Ayer, A. J., *Language, Truth and Logic*, London, 1947.

Ayer, A. J., *The Origins of Pragmatism*, London, 1968.

Bambrough, Renford, 'Plato's Political Analogies', in Peter Laslett (ed.), *Philosophy, Politics and Society*, Oxford, 1956.

Bradley, F. H., *Ethical Studies*, 2nd edn, Oxford, 1927.

Braithwaite, R. B., *An Empiricist's View of the Nature of Religious Belief*, Cambridge, 1955.

Butler, Joseph, *The Analogy of Religion*, edited by J. H. Bernard, London, 1900.

Butler, Joseph, *Sermons, Charges, Fragments and Correspondence*, edited by J. H. Bernard, London, 1900.

Clifford, W. K., 'The Ethics of Belief', in *Lectures and Essays*, vol. II, London, 1901.

Ewing, A. C., *The Definition of Good*, London, 1947.

Ewing, A. C., *Second Thoughts in Moral Philosophy*, London, 1959.

Hare, R. M., *The Language of Morals*, Oxford, 1952.

Hare, R. M., *Freedom and Reason*, Oxford, 1963.

Hare, R. M., 'The Objectivity of Values', *Common Factor*, June, 1964.

Hare, R. M., 'Geach: Good and Evil', in Philippa Foot (ed.), *Theories of Ethics*, Oxford, 1967.

Heller, Joseph, *Catch-22*, New York, 1955.

Hulme, T. E., *Further Speculations*, Minneapolis, 1955.

Hume, David, *A Treatise of Human Nature*, edited by L. A. Selby-Bigge, Oxford, 1888.

Hume, David, *Enquiries*, edited by L. A. Selby-Bigge, Oxford, 1902.

James, William, *The Will to Believe and Other Essays in Popular Philosophy*, New York, 1897.

Kant, Immanuel, *The Moral Law (The Groundwork of the Metaphysic of Morals)*, translated by H. J. Paton, London, 1948.

Kant, Immanuel, *Religion Within the Limits of Reason Alone*, New York, 1960.

Leavis, F. R., *The Common Pursuit*, London, 1952.

Lewis, C. I., *An Analysis of Knowledge and Valuation*, La Salle, Illinois, 1946.

Macdonald, Margaret, 'Ethics and the Ceremonial Use of Language', in Max Black (ed.), *Philosophical Analysis*, Englewood Cliffs, N.J., 1963.

Malcolm, Norman, *Dreaming*, London, 1959.

Mayo, Bernard, 'Commitments and Reasons', *Mind*, 1955.

Mill, J. S., *A System of Logic*, London, 1843.
B. Acton, London, 1972.

Moore, G. E., *Principia Ethica*, Cambridge, 1903.

Moore, G. E., 'A Defence of Common Sense', in *Philosophical Papers*, London, 1959.

Moore, G. E., 'Proof of an External World', in *Philosophical Papers*, London, 1959.

Murdoch, Iris, *The Sovereignty of Good*, London, 1970.

Newell, R. W., *The Concept of Philosophy*, London, 1967.

Nowell-Smith, P. H., *Ethics*, Harmondsworth, 1954.

Peirce, C. S., *Collected Papers*, vols I–VI, edited by Charles Hartshorne and Paul Weiss, Cambridge, Mass., 1931–5; vols VII–VIII, edited by Arthur Burks, Cambridge, Mass., 1958.

Peirce, C. S., *Values in a Universe of Chance*, edited by Philip P. Wiener, New York, 1958.

Phillips, D. Z. and H. O. Mounce, *Moral Practices*, London, 1970.

Prichard, H. A., *Moral Obligation*, Oxford, 1949.

Rashdall, Hastings, *The Theory of Good and Evil*, London, 1924.

Ross, W. D., *The Right and the Good*, Oxford, 1930.

Ross, W. D., *Foundations of Ethics*, Oxford, 1939.

Sartre, J.-P., *Existentialism and Humanism*, London, 1948.

Stevenson, C. L., *Ethics and Language*, New Haven, 1945.

Stevenson, C. L., *Facts and Values*, New Haven, 1963.

Williams, Bernard, *Problems of the Self*, Cambridge, 1973.

Wisdom, John, *Philosophy and Psycho-Analysis*, Oxford, 1953.

Wisdom, John, *Other Minds*, 2nd edn, Oxford, 1965.

Wisdom, John, *Paradox and Discovery*, Oxford, 1965.

Wisdom, John, 'The Virginia Lectures' (unpublished).

Wittgenstein, Ludwig, *Tractatus Logico-Philosophicus*, London, 1922.

Wittgenstein, Ludwig, *Philosophical Investigations*, Oxford, 1953.

Bibliographical Note

Professor John Wisdom lectured on Proof and Explanation at the University of Virginia in the Spring of 1957. A transcript of the lectures was prepared by Professor S. F. Barker and has circulated among friends and pupils of Professor Wisdom. A brief account of some of the themes of the lectures is given by Professor D. C. Yalden-Thomson in 'The Virginia Lectures' in Renford Bambrough (ed.), *Wisdom: Twelve Essays*, Oxford, 1974. It is to be hoped that the lectures will be published in due course. Meanwhile the most relevant of Wisdom's published writings to the themes of this book are 'Moore's Technique' and 'Metaphysics and Verification' in *Philosophy and Psycho-Analysis*, and 'A Feature of Wittgenstein's Technique' and 'Paradox and Discovery' in *Paradox and Discovery*.

Bernard Mayo's article, 'Commitments and Reasons' (*Mind*, 1955), is an exception to some statements made on pp. 111 and 113. I discovered this when the production of the book was too far advanced to allow the reference to be given in Chapter 7.

INDEX